Canon George Humphrey served five years in parishes in Norwich before teaching for some thirteen years in secondary schools in South Yorkshire (RE teacher at Mexborough Grammar School and later Head of PSE at Thurnscoe Comprehensive) and in Cheshire (Head of RE at Cheadle Grammar School). In 1980 he was appointed Adviser for religious education to the county and diocese of Gloucester, working in primary and secondary schools. For a number of years he worked as an OFSTED inspector in primary and secondary schools. In retirement he keeps contact with church schools as Bishop's Visitor and helps in his local community primary school.

George Humphrey

MONARCH
BOOKS

Oxford, UK & Grand Rapids, Michigan, USA

First published in 2005 by Monarch Books
(a publishing imprint of Lion Hudson plc),
Mayfield House, 256 Banbury Road, Oxford OX2 7DH
Tel: +44 (0) 1865 302750   Fax: +44 (0) 1865 302757
Email: monarch@lionhudson.com
www.lionhudson.com

Distributed by:
UK: Marston Book Services Ltd, PO Box 269,
Abingdon, Oxon OX14 4YN;
USA: Kregel Publications, PO Box 2607,
Grand Rapids, Michigan 49501.

UK ISBN 1 85424 678 X
US ISBN 0 8254 6078 6

British Library Cataloguing Data
A catalogue record for this book is available
from the British Library.

Book design by Lion Hudson plc.
Printed and bound in Great Britain by
Bookmarque Ltd, Croydon, Surrey

CONTENTS

INTRODUCTION

Though Luke is writing about the life of Jesus 2,000 years ago, his story has much in common with the concerns of any modern family. The family featured in these contemporary stories is the Robinson family, Steve and Kate and their three children, Peter (ten), Sarah (eight) and Jemma (six).

The themes of the stories that Luke writes are very similar to the themes that run through the daily life of the Robinsons. That's why these stories are in pairs – a story retold from Luke, linked with a story from the life of the Robinsons. The content of each story may be very different, but they share a common theme.

By hearing one of Luke's stories and then a story from the Robinsons (though ideally not on the same occasion), children will:

a) become familiar with some of the best stories from the Bible;

b) realise that the Bible is not just about things that happened 2,000 years ago to people living thousands of miles away, but that it also deals with issues that affect people today;

c) learn that ordinary families have problems that they can often solve with understanding and patience;

d) begin to appreciate that the Bible can help young people today to understand issues that affect their personal and social development as they grow to become responsible adults in society.

How to use the "Luke Out!" stories

The stories have been written with school assemblies in mind, though they could be used as part of personal and social education as required by the citizenship curriculum.

It is suggested that each of the pair of stories be used on separate occasions, though which of the pair is used first is a matter of personal choice.

The theme of each pair of stories is identified, with a few suggested questions for follow-up. The follow-up may be part of the daily assembly, but it might be used by the class teacher later, e.g. as part of circle time.

A brief prayer is included for use at school assembly.

SADNESS TURNED TO JOY
LUKE 1:5-25

THEME: **Happiness**

*Many things bring happiness, but sometimes we have to
wait patiently for them to happen.*

"Enough work for today," sighed Zechariah as he locked up his
workshop and started the long walk up the winding hill to his
house. "I wonder what Elizabeth has got for supper? That
chicken she cooked last week was better than anything you get
in the best hotels in Jerusalem." He whistled cheerfully as he
thought of the meal that would be waiting for him.

"Elizabeth, I'm back," he shouted as he took off his cloak.
Silence. "That's strange," he thought. "Elizabeth is usually here
wanting to know how the day has gone and who's paid their
bills and who hasn't. Where can she be?"

He searched everywhere and finally found her sitting
under the porch at the back of the house. He could tell something was wrong. She was sitting, staring into the distance,
with a sad look on her face. A tear began to trickle down her
cheek.

"Elizabeth, dear, what's the matter?" he cried, taking hold
of her hand.

"Oh, Zechariah," she wept, "I know I shouldn't be upset,
but when I saw Ruth across the road with her new baby, I just
couldn't help feeling so sad that we hadn't any children of our
own. All these years we've hoped and prayed that we would
have a baby and still we wait. It's not that I'm jealous of Ruth.
I feel so happy for her and Reuben her husband, but I do wish
we could have the same happiness."

"I know just how you feel, Elizabeth," sighed Zechariah.
"Hardly a day passes without me thinking how happy it would

make us both to have a child. God has blessed us in so many ways. Why doesn't he complete our happiness by giving us a child? Is it something we've done wrong, or is he trying to teach us to be happy just as we are?"

"We try to please God as best we can, and you a priest as well, serving him in the Temple in Jerusalem, as well as running your workshop here," argued Elizabeth.

They talked about nothing else all evening and were still trying to comfort each other as they climbed the stairs to bed.

Every year, when it was his turn to serve God in the Temple, Zechariah had to go to Jerusalem. This year was a special occasion because Zechariah had been chosen to burn incense in the holiest part of the Temple – a once-in-a-lifetime opportunity. No one else was allowed to go with him. While he was in the Temple, he prayed once more that God would bless Elizabeth and help her to have a baby. Zechariah was just about to leave when he got the shock of his life! At one side of the altar was an angel in dazzling white. Zechariah was startled, then terrified, then startled again!

"Don't be afraid, Zechariah," said the angel calmly. "I've been sent to tell you that God has answered your prayer. Elizabeth will have a baby and you are to call him John."

"But, but..." spluttered Zechariah, "how can this be true? We're both quite old now – it might be too late. Perhaps it's a mistake and I'm dreaming."

"Now look here," said the angel, just a little bit impatiently, "I am Gabriel and I've come straight from God. You've prayed all this time and now, when I tell you that God has answered your prayer, you start arguing with me! No more 'ifs' and 'buts'. You've said too much already. Because of this, you will not be able to speak another word until Elizabeth has had her baby. Perhaps that will teach you not to doubt God."

When his work at the Temple was finished, Zechariah couldn't wait to get home. He packed his few clothes, grabbed some food for the journey and set off as quickly as he could go.

What the angel had said was quite true. He rushed into the house, gave Elizabeth a big hug, opened his mouth to tell her the news – and, nothing! He spluttered and stuttered, but could not say a word.

"Now, Zechariah, just calm down and sit on this chair while I get you a drink," begged Elizabeth, wondering what on earth had happened to him.

It took Zechariah the rest of the evening to tell Elizabeth his good news. He got a loaf of bread and cradled it in his arms as if he was rocking a baby. He pointed upwards and put his hands together in prayer and then pointed to Elizabeth and did the baby-rocking all over again. At first Elizabeth did not know what to make of it, but slowly she realised that something special must have happened at the Temple. The joy on Zechariah's face, together with his frantic signs, told her that God had answered their prayers. For a long time Zechariah and Elizabeth kept this news to themselves. They were both so excited and so happy – but it was Elizabeth who did all the talking – Zechariah still couldn't say a word!

* * *

Stimulus questions

1. What sorts of things make you really happy?
2. Are they always *things you get* (e.g. presents, money, new clothes, toys), or are they things that *happen* to you or other people? (e.g. a friend gets better from an illness)
3. Can you think of when you had to wait a long time for something that made you happy?
4. How can other people tell that you are happy?

Thinking time

1. Think what Zechariah might have said to Elizabeth about their new baby if he had been able to speak.
2. Think of a time when you had to wait a long time for something that made you happy. How did you feel?

Prayer

"Lord, we thank you for the times when we have been very happy. Help us to be patient when we have to wait. Show us how we can bring happiness to other people by what we say and do. Amen."

JEMMA DOES IT AGAIN!

THEME: **Happiness**

What we say can make people feel very happy and sometimes make them feel very unhappy.

Breakfast time usually meant that everyone in the Robinson family was rushing around. Mr Robinson would be bolting a piece of toast and drinking a cup of tea at the same time, while glancing at the kitchen clock every 30 seconds and muttering under his breath, "I shall be late this morning." Peter, Sarah and Jemma would be gobbling cornflakes, making more slurping noises than usual. Mrs Robinson would be dashing here and there, bringing toast, clearing dishes and trying to remember the things the children needed to take to school.

Well, on this particular Friday morning, things were just as frantic as usual, except that Sarah, who was eight, was deep in thought, stirring her spoon round in her cornflakes with one hand and resting her head on the other.

"Mummy," she said thoughtfully, "why hasn't Mrs Dolman, my teacher, got any children? She looks about as old as you – and you and Daddy have got three of us."

"I don't know, darling," replied her Mum. "What a strange thing to ask just before you set off for school."

"Do you think they don't want any children?" continued Sarah.

"Perhaps they've seen what you three are like!" muttered Mr Robinson with a twinkle in his eye.

"I'm sure Mrs Dolman likes children," Mrs Robinson added quickly. "Just look how nice she is to you all when she's on playground duty."

"You're too young to know all about that sort of thing,"

Peter said scornfully. "You're only in Year 4 – you'll have to wait till you're in Year 6 to see the video and listen to the school nurse explaining it all." Peter enjoyed showing how much more he knew than his two sisters.

"Well, I think Mr and Mrs Dolman are probably very sad not to have children," insisted Sarah, completely ignoring Peter's last remark.

All this time, Jemma, who was only six, and just in the Year 2 class, said nothing. She stopped eating, looked first at Sarah and then at Peter and then at her mum and dad. She was thinking hard, but saying nothing!

Mrs Robinson collected the children from school at half past three, though Peter always walked about ten paces in front of them – he thought he was far too old to be collected from school. Jemma was bursting with excitement but nobody took any notice. It was when they were having tea that Jemma could not contain herself any longer.

"I know why Mrs Dolman hasn't got any children," she burst out, "because I asked her when she was in the playground this morning."

"You did *what*?" exclaimed her mother.

"Oh, Jemma, what have you done?" sighed Peter.

"Oh, Jemma, what have you done?" echoed Sarah.

"Well, at breakfast no one seemed to know, and you're always saying that if we don't know something we should ask someone who does. I felt sure that Mrs Dolman would know," pleaded Jemma, wondering what all the fuss was about. "She said it was kind of me to ask, but it wasn't the right time yet. What did she mean by that?"

Mr Robinson sighed, but kept reading the sports page in the newspaper.

"I'm sure you meant well, Jemma," explained her mother, "but that's not the sort of thing you just go up to someone and ask – it might have made Mrs Dolman feel more unhappy than ever."

Jemma tried to understand, and really did hope that Mrs Dolman wasn't upset by what she had asked.

Mrs Robinson wondered what she could do to put things right. Jemma always wanted to do the right thing, but very often it didn't work out as she intended. When the children had gone to bed, Mrs Robinson chatted things over with Mr Robinson and then telephoned Mrs Dolman.

"Hello, Mrs Dolman, it's Mrs Robinson, Jemma's mother. I'm terribly sorry about what Jemma said to you, but she really meant no harm and is quite upset to think that she might have said the wrong thing and made you very unhappy," explained Mrs Robinson.

They chatted for a few minutes and then Mrs Robinson finished the call with, "Well, fancy that! If you're sure it's all right, I'll give the children, especially Jemma, a big surprise in the morning!"

The following morning, being Saturday, there wasn't the usual frantic rush at breakfast. When Mr Robinson was on his second piece of toast and Peter on his second bowl of cornflakes, Mrs Robinson looked at them all with a broad smile.

"Well, I've something to tell you all," she said proudly. "I telephoned Mrs Dolman last night to explain about Jemma, and guess what – she is going to have a baby and we are the first people she's told! Mr and Mrs Dolman are so happy!"

"Oh Mummy!" cried Jemma. "I'm so pleased. I'll give Mrs Dolman a big smile when I go to school on Monday, but I promise I won't ask her any more questions!"

* * *

Stimulus questions

1. What sorts of things can people say that make other people unhappy?

2. What sorts of things can people say that make other people happy?
3. Why do you think that having children makes most parents very happy?
4. How can people, who don't have children of their own, still show that they like children? (e.g. adopt, foster, be good "aunties" and "uncles", help with children's clubs and organisations.)

Thinking time

1. Think of a time when you made someone very happy by what you said. How did you feel? How do you think they felt?
2. Think of a time when you made someone very unhappy by what you said. What could you have said instead?

Prayer

"Lord, we know that what we say can make people very happy and sometimes make them very unhappy. Forgive us when we have made people sad. Help us to bring happiness to others by what we say and do. Amen."

HIS NAME IS JOHN
LUKE 1:57-80

THEME: **The Individual**

Although everyone is born into a family, their name makes them an individual.

Elizabeth and Zechariah were so thrilled that after waiting so long they were finally going to have a baby, just as the angel in the Temple had said. They were not the only ones to be excited. Everyone in their village shared their happiness and behaved as though a new baby was going to be born into their family.

At the village shop they talked of nothing else for weeks.

"Two loaves, please, and have you heard the good news about Elizabeth? She's going to have a baby."

"Oh yes, it'll be so nice for them both after all this time. I expect they thought they would never have any children."

"Yes, after all this time. I suppose they will be hoping that it will be a boy. Then they can call him Zechariah after his father."

"I don't imagine they will mind, so long as the baby is strong and healthy. If it's a girl then they'll surely call her Elizabeth after her mother."

It was no different at the village inn.

"Have you heard the latest, Ben? Old Zechariah's going to be a father!"

"Well, I never. After all these years! Who would have thought that he'd have to get used to being wakened by a baby crying in the middle of the night?"

"Yes, it's going to be hard for them both at their age."

"Still, I don't suppose they mind at all; they look so happy and so much younger!"

"I expect they will be hoping it's a boy. Then they can call him Zechariah after his father."

"Or if it's a girl, they'll surely call her Elizabeth after her mother."

So they went on. Whenever and wherever people in the village met, they talked of only one thing – the new baby. The women were busy making baby clothes and they soon had enough shawls and blankets for half a dozen babies. All the village carpenters had the idea of making a cradle. In the end they had a meeting to decide who should do it and what else the others could make. About one thing they were all quite certain – if it was a boy he should be called Zechariah, and if it was a girl she should be called Elizabeth. Nobody thought to ask what Elizabeth and Zechariah thought!

The day finally arrived for the baby to be born, and all the villagers gathered round the house waiting for news and chatting excitedly about whether it was going to be a girl or a boy.

When the door of the house slowly opened and the nurse stepped out, a hush descended over the crowd and you could have heard a pin drop.

"It's a boy," she shouted with joy, "and mother and baby are very well!"

A cheer went up and they all started singing and dancing in the streets.

"Baby Zechariah! Baby Zechariah!" they chanted. It was getting quite dark before the last villagers had made their way home.

Eight days after the baby was born, everyone gathered together again for the special ceremony to thank God for the baby and to give him his name. The rabbi took the baby in his arms and without asking its parents, started to say in a loud voice, "I name this child Zech..." when Elizabeth grabbed his arm and said, "No, he is to be called **John**."

For a moment there was a startled hush. Then uproar broke out:

"You can't call him John! He's to be Zechariah after his father!"

"Where did you get the idea of calling him John?"

"There's no one in your family called John – why call him that?"

"It's expected that the first boy in a family is called after his father!"

"You ask old Zechariah. He'll tell you that he wants the baby named after him!"

Zechariah was speechless – as he had been since the angel in the Temple told him that Elizabeth would have a baby. He asked them to bring him a writing tablet. They all crowded round to see what he would write. It was so quiet they could hear the squeaky pen as he slowly wrote, "His name is **J–0–H–N**." At once Zechariah was able to speak again, and he shouted with joy, "His name is **John**, his name is **John**."

He took the baby in his arms and sang out, "Praise be to the Lord God of Israel. You, my son, will be a special servant of God to prepare for the one who will come to save us."

Well, what could they say? "John" was what Zechariah said, and "John" he was called!

As the crowd made their way home they said to one another, "He may be the son of Zechariah and Elizabeth, but by calling him John we shall know that he is a very special person."

* * *

Stimulus questions

1. Why did the people think that the baby would be called Elizabeth or Zechariah?
2. Which of you are named after a member of your family? Who?

3. Is any one named after someone famous? (footballer, pop star)
4. Why do you think that parents sometimes name their children after a member of the family, or someone famous?
5. When babies are baptised (christened) in church, the minister only uses their Christian name (Alison, David) not their family name (Alison Smith, David Johnson). Why?
6. When you grow up and if you have children, what will you call them? Why?

Thinking time

1. Think of your own name. Think of ways in which you are the same as other members of your family, and ways you are different from them (physical features, interests, hobbies, etc.).
2. Look at your fingertips. No one else in the world has exactly the same pattern as you. This makes you very special.

Prayer

"Lord, thank you for making me just as I am. Help me to be the best I can. Forgive me when I say and do things wrong and help me to be more like you want me to be. Amen."

JEMMA'S TEDDY LOSKIE

THEME: **The Individual**

Everyone has an important part to play, however young.

The Robinson family were going to spend the weekend at the seaside in a caravan. Mrs Robinson had been able to finish work early and so everything was packed and ready when Peter, Sarah and Jemma got home from school. They had just to wait for Mr Robinson to arrive from work so they could load the car. It was nearly six o'clock when he arrived. He looked tired and rather bad-tempered.

"It's always the same when we're planning to go somewhere," he grumbled. "First the telephone rang just as I was about to leave the office, and then there was a big queue of traffic stretching for miles before the roundabout."

"Daddy, you know when we went to the caravan last time?" piped up Jemma.

"Yes, Jemma," snapped Mr Robinson.

"Well, you know we passed a shop that sold nothing but teddy bears," she continued.

"Yes, Jemma," sighed Mr Robinson, knowing what was coming next.

"Well, you said that next time we went to the caravan we could stop and look at all the teddies. Well, this is next time," she said, looking pleadingly at her father.

"There'll be no time for looking at teddies; it'll be dark before we get to the caravan as it is; anyway the shops will all be closed," he said finally.

At last the car was loaded and the three children were bundled into the back seat. They could tell that Dad was still in a bad mood, the way he changed gear sharply and banged on the brakes at traffic lights. The roads were so busy; it seemed that everyone was going to the seaside for the weekend. Jemma noticed the teddy bear shop as they sped past. There were lights on and people inside, but she knew there was no point mentioning it again. By the time they arrived and made their way down the farm track to where the caravan was it was dark.

"You all wait in the car until I've opened the caravan and put some lights on," ordered their father. "I won't be long, once I find the key."

But Mr Robinson was long – so long that they wondered what was wrong. Sarah and Jemma (who was only six) were very tired and Peter was cross. Mr Robinson finally stormed back to the car and stuck his head through the window.

"I couldn't get the key in the lock and I dropped it, and now I've lost the key!" he grumbled.

"What does Daddy say?" wailed Jemma. "He's *loskie*?"

"He's *lost the key*, silly girl," shouted Peter at Jemma.

"I thought he said 'loskie'," whimpered Jemma, "and I didn't know what 'loskie' meant." She felt tears coming into her eyes, but was determined not to cry, especially in front of Peter.

"Come on, out you all get and see if you can find the key," ordered Mr Robinson.

Jemma was just about to shuffle out of the car when her father snapped at her, "Not you, Jemma. We've enough trouble trying to find a key without having to find a six-year-old."

Jemma sank back into the car seat. She was feeling very unhappy. First Daddy didn't keep his promise about visiting the teddy shop, then Peter shouted at her for no reason and now Daddy says she's no help, just trouble. She wished she could slide down between the seats and vanish completely.

After a long time they all trooped back to the car. They had clearly not found the key.

"I'll have to walk down to the farm and borrow a torch," said Mr Robinson, and off he went.

Mrs Robinson started to read a magazine, Peter got out his latest Harry Potter book and Sarah picked up her puzzle book. Jemma was quiet and just thought. She slowly pulled on the door handle and as it opened she slid out and crept over to the caravan. It was only a few steps from the car and Mrs Robinson kept a watchful eye on her.

As she looked first in the grass and then among the pebbles, she hummed to herself:

> "Now little lost key,
> Where can you be?
> I'll get down on one knee,
> And then I shall see."

Just then the moon came from behind the clouds and she saw something glinting in the moonlight. It was very small and wedged between two large pebbles. She stretched her hand as far as she could and her tiny fingers just reached. She pulled it out and sure enough it was a key. She rushed back to the car, peered through the window and said, "Mummy, is this what Daddy was looking for?"

"Jemma, you are a treasure! Let's get into the caravan and get some supper ready. Daddy will be so pleased!"

Jemma wasn't so sure about the last part, but when her father came back with a torch, he was so surprised to see them cooking fish fingers and beans and getting their things unpacked. Mrs Robinson explained how Jemma had found the key, and without saying anything Daddy gave Jemma a big hug.

"I may only be six, but I'm a good finder and I've got little fingers to reach tiny things," she explained.

"Jemma," said Daddy, "you've done something that none of us was able to do – you really are a treasure. First thing tomorrow I'm going into town to buy a torch to keep in the car. Would you like to come with me?"

"Yes, please," she replied eagerly. She knew that she might get to look at the teddies, after all.

Daddy and Jemma were back before lunch the next day. Mr Robinson carried a fine-looking torch and Jemma was tightly holding a teddy, dressed in a swimsuit.

"What are you going to call your new teddy?" enquired Sarah.

"That's easy," said Jemma with a broad smile. "He's called **'Loskie'**."

"'Loskie'?" said Sarah with a puzzled expression on her face. "What does that mean?"

"Oh, I get it!" said Peter proudly. "You're a very smart girl, Jemma."

"Yes," said Dad smiling, " a special girl too. What would we have done without her?"

* * *

Stimulus questions

1. What things had made Jemma so unhappy?
2. Why was she such an important member of her family, even though she was only six?
3. Can you think of a time when you did something that no one else could do?

Thinking time

1. Think of a time when you were very unhappy because grown-ups were cross with you. How did you feel?
2. Think of a time when you did something special for your family. How did you feel?

Prayer

"Lord, thank you for making each of us special. Thank you for giving us gifts and skills. Show us how to use them to help other people. Amen."

THE BIRTH OF JESUS
LUKE 1:26-38; 2:1-7

THEME: **Trust**

Difficulties can be overcome with trust and patience.

Mary and Joseph were so excited about getting married. They both lived in Nazareth, so they were able to see each other quite often and begin to make plans for their new home. Joseph was a carpenter and spent all his spare time making furniture, while Mary was busy making clothes for the wedding and other things for the house. They were very happy and their plans for the future seemed so straightforward. But this didn't last for long.

Mary was alone in the house, quietly getting on with her work, when suddenly she was dazzled by a bright light. As she rubbed her eyes, she heard a voice.

"Mary," it said, "I am Gabriel and God has sent me to tell you that you are going to have a baby that you must call Jesus. He will be great and will be called the Son of God. You have been chosen to be the mother of this very special baby."

At first Mary was speechless, then all sorts of things rushed into her head. "Why me?" she thought. "Why am I so special? And as if I haven't got enough on my mind thinking about the wedding without having to plan for a baby! It's all too much – and what am I going to tell Joseph?" It was a long time before Mary felt calmer. "Perhaps this baby is the one that God promised to send to save us and show us how to serve God. How wonderful that God has chosen me to bring up this baby. With God's help I'll be the best mother I can! Oh, but what *am* I going to tell Joseph?"

When Mary and Joseph met next day, each of them knew something had happened. Mary looked at Joseph and then quickly looked away. Joseph looked at Mary and then quickly looked away!

"What's the matter?" they both said together.

"You first, Mary," spluttered Joseph with a deep frown spreading across his brow.

"W-e-ll," began Mary, and in a quiet voice and trying hard to look at Joseph, she told him all that the angel had said. When she got to the part about having a baby and calling him Jesus, she was surprised to see the frown on Joseph's brow disappear and in its place a big smile stretching from ear to ear!

"That's amazing," Joseph said excitedly. "Last night I had a dream in which an angel told me exactly the same thing – I just didn't know how I was going to tell you! It's not going to be easy for us, Mary, but with God's help we shall be the best parents we can for this special baby." They held hands and walked down the road chattering excitedly about everything the angels had told them.

One evening Joseph came home from work with a worried look on his face.

"What is it, Joseph?" asked Mary. "You've not lost the order for that new plough, have you? We could do with the extra money just now."

"No, Mary, it's worse than that – a lot worse," he replied with a sigh. "A Roman official arrived this morning and put up a notice to say that the emperor is ordering everyone to go to their home town and register their names. It sounds harmless enough but he wants to know exactly how many people there are so that no one can avoid paying taxes."

"It couldn't have happened at a worse time," said Mary. "We've got everything ready for the baby."

"I know," agreed Joseph, "and I shall have to go to Bethlehem – it's more than 100 kilometres (70 miles). It'll take me days and days to get there and back. All that way and just to register my name. What about you? Who's going to look after you?"

"Don't you worry about me," Mary stated firmly. "I'm coming with you!"

"But what about the baby?" protested Joseph. "You're in no state to be making such a long journey – who knows exactly how long it will take us?"

"Joseph, have you forgotten what the angels said?" she replied gently. "God will be with us as we travel."

"You're right, Mary," agreed Joseph. "Doing God's will is never easy, but if we stay together, then with his help we shall be all right, whatever happens."

So they packed their things and set off for Bethlehem. It *was* hard and even though Mary travelled on a donkey, each day she became more and more tired. Joseph did all he could to make her comfortable and they managed to find somewhere to stay each night – until they got to Bethlehem! The place was swarming with people, all wanting to register their names. Bethlehem was the ancient city of great King David and so there were thousands of people flocking there. They trudged around every inn looking for a place to stay, but it was the same everywhere they went. Crowds packed into every space and the noise was deafening. Everybody was having a good time; it was more like a holiday camp with crowds celebrating their ancestor King David. But it wasn't much of a holiday for Mary and Joseph.

"What are we going to do, Mary?" said Joseph anxiously. "We must find somewhere for the night. Even if we do find space in one of the inns, all that noise and shouting and dancing is not going to be easy for you – certainly no place for a baby to be born."

"Joseph, you've done everything you can to help," said Mary, "but God must know what he's doing."

"You're right, again, Mary. Let's try one more inn," said Joseph determinedly.

"Sorry, we're full to bursting," said the innkeeper. Then, noticing Mary, he added, "But we've got a barn at the back, with plenty of warm straw, and I'm sure the animals won't make half the noise of this lot in here!"

They were very thankful for the offer and settled down for the night surrounded by sheep and cows. So it was that Jesus was born.

"Who would have thought that God's Son would be born in a stable?" smiled Mary. "But God kept his promise to me. This is a very special child."

"We never thought it would turn out like this," added Joseph, "but we are all together, and I feel sure God will look after his holy family."

* * *

Stimulus questions

1. What things would Mary and Joseph have to plan for their wedding?
2. What sort of things would they have to prepare for the baby?
3. What helped them to cope with all their problems?
4. Think of something that was very difficult for you. How did you manage?

Thinking time

1. Think of a time when you had to face something that was very hard. How did you manage? Which people helped you? What did they do to help?

Prayer

"Lord, when we face something that is very hard for us to cope with, help us to look for help from those we love and trust. Amen."

STAYING TOGETHER

THEME: **Trust**

Difficulties can be overcome if people trust each other and work together.

"Let's play 'Do you remember when...'" said Peter as they set off on the long journey to visit Grandma Taylor.

"Do you remember," said Sarah, "when cousin Ben came to Wales with us last year and we climbed Mount Snowdon?"

They all remembered that holiday, especially the day they decided to climb up Mount Snowdon. It was bright and sunny when they set off from the caravan, but when they got to the car park at the bottom of the mountain there were a few clouds in the sky.

"I think it will still be safe," said Mr Robinson looking at the clouds. "We've all got warm coats and strong shoes and the weather forecast for this afternoon is quite good. The really important thing is that we all keep together; no racing off trying to be the first," he added, looking especially at Peter and Ben. Ben was usually quite sensible and did what he was told, but although he was only about a year older than Peter, he thought he was so grown-up now that he was at secondary school and Peter was only in Year 6 at primary school. He just had to show that he could run faster, swim quicker, climb higher and kick a football further than Peter. He was determined that he was going to be first to the top of Mount Snowdon.

They set off, walking by the side of the railway track that went right to the top of the mountain. "It will be longer this way," said Mr Robinson, "but it is easier, and we shall be sure of the way, especially if the weather turns nasty. But we must all keep together."

Everything was fine at first; even Jemma, who was only six, managed to keep up with them and passed the time by counting the railway sleepers until she couldn't count any further. Ben and Peter were keen to press on, but remembered what Peter's Dad had said about keeping together. They stopped about halfway up for some sandwiches and a bottle of juice and then set off again. Jemma was getting rather tired, but didn't complain. As they got nearer the top they noticed that it was getting misty and they couldn't see very far ahead. The railway track was easy to follow and there were lots of other people walking up with them.

It was then that Ben had the idea that if he was to be sure of being the first to the top he might just as well get a little way ahead. Nobody noticed at first that Ben wasn't with them. They had their heads down to shield against the wind, and the mist was getting thicker. It was Jemma who cried out, "Where's Ben?" She was usually the first to notice when something was different.

"He was with us a minute ago," said Mrs Robinson.

"He was just ahead of me for a long time," added Peter.

"Daddy did tell us all to keep together," commented Sarah.

"Oh dear," sighed Mr Robinson, "this is the last thing we want with this mist – and I did say that everything would be fine if we all kept together."

It wasn't long before they arrived at the top and quickly made for the café and a hot drink – and to meet up with Ben. The café was very crowded and people were jostling to get to the front of the queue. They searched for a long time and were quite sure that Ben was not there. They even shouted his name above the noise, but no one replied.

"What do you think we should do?" asked Mrs Robinson. They all had different ideas, but they were agreed on one thing – that this would not have happened if they had all kept together. They finally decided that Mrs Robinson and Jemma would go back on the train to see if Ben had already got to the bottom. Mr Robinson, Peter and Sarah would begin to walk down, following the track and hoping to find Ben. They walked in silence for about ten minutes, keeping close together to shelter from the wind, which was getting stronger, but keeping a sharp lookout for Ben. Two or three times they saw a shadowy figure in the mist just ahead of them that they thought was Ben, but each time they shouted "Ben!" and went up to the person, they were met by a puzzled-looking stranger.

It was Sarah who first spotted the faint outline of a figure crouching behind a large rock. As they got nearer they could tell the figure was shivering and crying. "Ben!" shouted Mr Robinson. At once the bowed head of the figure straightened up and they all breathed a sigh of relief when they saw it was Ben. He was shivering and looked very pale; he managed to wipe his eyes quickly as he struggled to stand up.

"Oh, Ben," cried Mr Robinson, "we're so glad to have found you. Are you all right?"

Ben at once started to explain what had happened and how sorry he was for the worry he had caused, but Mr Robinson, wrapping his own scarf round Ben's neck, interrupted, "That's all right, Ben, we're just glad you're safe. You can tell us all about it when we get back to the car." With his arm round Ben, and the others hand in hand, they were at the bottom of the mountain in no time.

Mrs Robinson and Jemma were waiting at the station, but of course it was Jemma who spotted the others.

"Mummy, they're here – all of them – and Ben!" Everybody was trying to talk at the same time, but when they had all finished giving Ben hugs, they piled into the car and were soon feeling warmer.

"I'm very sorry for what I've done," said Ben weakly. "I so wanted to be the first to the top, but I wasn't sure which way to go and decided to wait for you to catch up. You must have passed me without noticing me."

"So you haven't been to the top after all?" enquired Peter.

"No," admitted Ben, "and I didn't do as I was told, and I caused you a lot of worry, and I don't expect you will ever invite me on holiday again."

"Well," said Mr Robinson, "you seem to have learned your lesson. I'm sure we shall want you to come with us again next year – I shall need someone strong to carry the rucksack," he added with a smile.

"And if we all stay together," piped up Jemma, " we might be able to climb Mount Everest one day!"

They all laughed, but they knew she was right about staying together.

*   *   *

Stimulus questions

1. What do you think Ben was thinking about as he crouched behind the rock?
2. What big lessons did Ben learn from his experience?
3. Have you ever been lost? What happened? How were you found?

Thinking time

1. Think of a time when you got lost. How did you feel? How were you found? How did you feel then?

Prayer

"Lord, when we get lost, keep us strong and show us how to trust those who can really help us. Amen."

THE SHEPHERDS
LUKE 2:8-20

THEME: **Wonder and Mystery**
There are many things in life we don't fully understand.

"What a way to spend your life – watching sheep!" grumbled Dan as he settled down against a tree trunk for yet another night.

"You know why we're here, Dan," said Reuben. "It's to guard the animals against thieves and wolves; you'd have something to grumble about if half the flock was stolen and the other half went to feed hungry wolves."

"I know you're right, Reuben, as usual, but you must agree it's not exactly thrilling to be out here night after night just watching sheep. When did we last have trouble with thieves? And the fire keeps the wolves well away. Just think of all the fun we could be having in the village – you can even hear the singing and dancing up here on the hills."

"There'll be plenty of time for singing and dancing when we have to take the flocks down to the village for the winter. It's such good grazing up here on the hills – and it's so peaceful and quiet. Just look at that black sky, with hundreds of stars twinkling in the darkness."

"There you go again, Reuben – before long you'll be composing songs and singing them just like our ancestor David did when he was out on the hills looking after his father's sheep. Anyway, it's all right for you – you're an old man and the idea of sitting watching sheep all night might be your idea of excitement, but it's not mine! I want thrills and excitement and a bit of mystery – this is about the last place on earth where any of that is going to happen!" With that, Dan put some more wood on the fire, wrapped his cloak round his shoulders and with a sigh of boredom settled down with his back against a tree.

Moments later, without any warning, the sky lit up, brighter than a hot summer's day. Dan and Reuben and the other shepherds were so startled and blinded by the bright light that they fell about on top of each other in their haste to grab their shepherds' staffs. Dan, being a young man, was first on his feet. He was so scared that already beads of sweat were trickling down his neck and face. No sooner had he helped Reuben to his feet than he heard a booming voice:

"Don't be afraid – I've brought you good news that will fill you with joy."

"W–w–what is it?" gasped Dan.

"This very night, in Bethlehem the city of David, a baby has been born who will be the Saviour of the world!" the angel went on.

"Where has this happened and how do we know we're not just dreaming?" questioned Dan.

"You will find a baby lying in a manger," the angel continued, and before Dan could say another word the whole sky seemed to be full of angels singing louder than any choir.

"Glory to God in the highest, and on earth peace to all those on whom his favour rests," they sang.

Just as quickly as they had arrived, the angels disappeared, leaving Dan and the others groping around until their eyes got used to the darkness again.

"Well, I hope you're satisfied now," smiled Reuben looking at Dan, who was still nervously wiping his forehead. "Is that the sort of thrills and excitement you wanted?"

"It's a mystery all right," murmured Dan. "What does it all mean, and why us?"

"I just wonder," replied Reuben thoughtfully. "It was you who talked about David composing songs out on these hills, wasn't it? Well, in one of his songs he said that God would hear the prayers of the humble and lowly, and there's none so humble and lowly as shepherds. We've had the excitement and thrills; now let's see if we can solve the mystery."

They made sure the sheep were safe and set off at once for Bethlehem.

"The only clue we've got is a baby in a manger!" said Dan excitedly. "What is a newly-born baby doing in an animal's feeding trough?"

It was wise old Reuben who worked out that the baby must belong to a couple who had come to Bethlehem to register along with lots of other people, and that since all the inns were very busy, perhaps the only room they could find was in a stable belonging to one of the inns. Of course, he was right, and after a lot of careful detective work, they found the stable. They knocked quietly on the stable door and peeped in. They saw Mary and Joseph and sure enough in one of the feeding troughs they spotted the baby.

"It's the best we could do for a cradle," explained Joseph, "and Mary is able to get some rest here away from the crowds. But how did you know we were here?"

Mary and Joseph were amazed when Dan and Reuben told them what had happened while they were looking after their sheep. The shepherds took one last look at Jesus in the manger and then quietly said goodbye. They went back to their sheep, singing and dancing and praising God. They told everyone they met what had happened.

"Well, Dan, you wanted thrills, excitement and mystery, and that's just what you got," beamed Reuben.

"Wow," exclaimed Dan, "that's enough excitement for one night. I wonder how all this will work out, and what will become of the baby when he grows up."

* * *

Stimulus questions

1. What might the shepherds have thought had happened when the bright light shone at night?
2. Did Dan get the excitement he wanted? How?
3. What are some of the great wonders of the world in which we live? What does it make you feel about the world?
4. What might Dan have thought would happen to baby Jesus when he grew up?

Thinking time

1. Think of something that is really wonderful about our world. How does it make you feel?

Prayer

"Lord, we thank you for all the wonderful things in the world. We thank you for the birth of Jesus. Help us to be keen to learn about what we don't yet understand. Amen."

WONDER AND MYSTERY

THEME: **Wonder and Mystery**
There are many things that show us that we live in a wonderful world.

It wasn't very often that Peter and Sarah Robinson were allowed to stay up late, especially during the week, but this particular Wednesday night was special. It was part of the Christmas Fayre at the village hall. There were stalls with Christmas decorations, used toys and games that people no longer wanted, raffles, lucky dips and lots to eat and drink. Their Dad went with them, while Mum stayed at home to look after Jemma, who was only six.

They had a good time at the Fayre. Peter bought a computer game and Sarah some decorations for the Christmas tree. They all enjoyed the cake and mince pies and drank enough juice to make them ready to burst. It was quite late when Mr Robinson reminded them that it was school in the morning and they had better go home.

As they left the noise and the very warm and stuffy atmosphere inside the hall and stepped outside into the quiet, cold night air, they buttoned up their coats as the frost stung their cheeks and nipped their nose and ears.

"Wow! Just look up at the sky," cried Sarah. "I've never seen so many stars. There must be hundreds and hundreds – and they look so near that you could reach out and scoop up a handful!"

"Huh!" said Peter scornfully. "Actually, astronomers reckon that there could be 10,000 billion billion stars in the universe – there's a lot more than the ones you can see." Peter knew a lot about the planets and stars. He had books galore at home about astronomy and he got a telescope for his last birthday. He spent a lot of time reading about things like asteroids, quasars, comets and black holes. He took the opportunity to put Sarah right about a few things.

"Did you know," he went on, "that the nearest real star is called Proxima Centauri. It's so far away that if you went in a car at 100 kilometres per hour it would take you 50 million years to reach it!"

"Well, that might be true, but they look so small and pretty, it's just as though someone took a handful of tiny jewels and threw them across a blanket of black velvet," replied Sarah, not letting Peter's facts and figures spoil her wonder at the magnificent sky.

"When we go to the family service at church we sing a song that says, 'He that flung stars into space'," said Mr Robinson, trying hard to get a word in.

"Yes," added Sarah, "and we are learning a song that says, 'Make me a star to lighten the darkness'."

"But they're only songs! Actually," went on Peter, like some robot reeling off a list of statistics, "the stars and planets are not small at all. The diameter of the Sun is about 1,392,500 kilometres and it weighs about 500 times more than all the other planets put together. It doesn't look it, but the Sun is a lot bigger than the Earth; a bit like a beach ball compared to a ping-pong ball. The Sun is very hot – about 5,500 degrees Celsius and it burns up 4,000 tonnes of hydrogen every second."

Sarah ignored this latest set of facts and figures.

"Look how some of the stars group together to make pretty patterns," she said excitedly.

"That's right, Sarah," said her father encouragingly, "they've got special names. That one over there is called The Plough. It looks a bit like an old-fashioned plough. Follow the end two stars until you come to a very bright one – that's called Polaris and always points north. In ancient times sailors used that for navigation."

"Actually," butted in Peter again, "they only seem to be grouped together; they are really many light years apart."

"What's a 'light year'?" enquired Sarah, though she knew she was asking for trouble the moment she asked the question.

"Well, actually," replied Peter, "a light year is the distance that light travels in a whole year."

This didn't mean very much to Sarah, so she didn't ask Peter any more questions.

"Daddy," said Sarah, "whatever I say about the stars, Peter says something different. Who's right, me or Peter?"

"Well, I think you are both right," replied Mr Robinson with a sigh. "Peter knows a lot about astronomy, so I'm sure his facts are correct, but what the stars and planets make you think about and how they make you feel is also important. We are human beings with thoughts and feelings, not just computers that churn out information."

"Looking at the sky makes me feel very, very small," added Sarah, encouraged by what her father had just said, "and it makes me think that we have been given the job of looking after our beautiful world so that it isn't spoiled. When we get home I'm going to write a poem about how the sky makes me feel."

"I think I'll make a chart of our solar system," said Peter, not wanting to be outdone. "What are you going to do, Dad?"

"Well, I'm going to make your Mum and me a nice cup of tea, and then get your milk and biscuits ready for bed – so your charts and poems will have to wait for another day! It's school in the morning."

Sarah yawned and rubbed her eyes. Peter tried not to yawn, but he was feeling just as tired as Sarah. They walked the rest of the way home in silence, each of them thinking about what their Dad had said – how could they both be right?

*　*　*

Stimulus questions

1. Who do you think had the right ideas about the sky, Sarah or Peter? Why?
2. Can you think of a time when you saw some wonder of nature that made you say, "Wow!"? What was it?
3. Sarah said the sky made her think that people had been given the job of looking after our planet. Do you agree? How can we do it?

Thinking time

1. Think of a time when you saw some wonder of nature. How did it make you feel?

Prayer

"Lord, you have given us a wonderful world. Make us keen to learn all about it and determined to take care of it. Amen."

THE PROMISE TO SIMEON
LUKE 2:21-38

THEME: **Keeping Promises**
We have to be patient for some promises to be kept.

On the corner, just outside the carpenter's shop, a small group of old men were sitting on a bench eagerly talking. They met there every day, exchanging the latest news and solving the world's problems.

"Where's Simeon today?" asked Reuben. "He's usually here by this time."

"He's not been looking well these last few weeks," said Dan. "Perhaps there's something on his mind that's troubling him."

"Well, this is the place to get his problems solved," added Jacob. "Why doesn't he ask us?"

"Perhaps he will," said Reuben. "Isn't this him coming now?"

Reuben was right; it was Simeon slowly making his way through the crowds. His head was bowed, almost hiding the worried look on his face. He was late this morning because he had spent more than his usual length of time at his prayers. All his long life he had said his prayers each day, either at home or in the synagogue. Since he lived in Jerusalem he would often visit the great Temple and spend hours there thinking and praying. Everyone liked him because he not only spent time praying, he also did everything he could to help people and took time to listen to them. Today he needed someone to listen to him.

"Hello, Simeon," said Dan, "you look a bit sad this morning – what's troubling you?"

"Well, Dan, it's good of you to ask," replied Simeon. "There is something on my mind. I've not told anyone about this, but I know I can trust you." Reuben and Jacob gathered round Simeon as he told his story to Dan.

"You know that for many years our nation has been waiting for God to send another great prophet to show us God's way. But nothing has happened and things are getting worse and worse. Well, many years ago, while I was praying in the Temple, something very strange happened to me. I felt that God was telling me that he would send a Saviour and that I would live to see him. But I'm getting very old now and I surely can't live much longer, and yet nothing has happened. It's not like God not to keep his promise."

"It's no good blaming God," said Reuben. "Perhaps it's you that's got it all wrong."

"Reuben's right," added Jacob. "It's easy to get carried away and to think all sorts of things when you are in the Temple. I sometimes wonder if you spend too much time there, praying all the time and worrying about all the things that are wrong in the world."

"But I only do what I think God wants me to do," explained Simeon, "and I was so sure that God had promised that I would see his Saviour."

"Well, I believe that God keeps his promises," said Dan encouragingly. "There's surely time yet – you could easily live another few years. That gives God plenty of time. I'm sure he's not forgotten."

"It's kind of you to say that," replied Simeon. "I must learn to be more patient." With that, Simeon went off to the market to do his shopping.

Some days later Simeon went to the Temple to pray. He had only been there a few minutes when he noticed that a young couple came in carrying a baby wrapped up tightly in a shawl. They had probably come to thank God for their baby and to ask him to bless him. As they came near to Simeon, the strangest feeling came over him. His heart beat faster; he felt a tingling sensation running up and down his spine. The couple brought the baby right over to him and smiled at Simeon. It was then that Simeon knew what the strange feeling was about. He asked the mother if he could hold the baby. Taking him in his arms, and with a broad smile on his radiant face, Simeon looked up and said, "Lord, you have kept your promise to me. I've seen with my own eyes the Saviour you have sent to us and to all the people on earth. I'm now ready to die, the happiest man in the world."

Handing the baby back he said to the baby's mother, "You must be very happy to have this special baby. He is the one that God has sent to show us God's way. Many will believe God because of him, but others will turn against him. As well as great happiness he will also bring you sadness."

Mary and Joseph (because these were the names of the baby's parents, of course) were amazed and didn't quite know what to make of it all. As they made their way home, they talked together about what Simeon had said.

The next morning Simeon was up extra early and made his way down to where he knew Dan, Reuben and Jacob would already be exchanging the latest news. When they saw him, they could tell from his beaming face that he had some more news for them.

"You're looking happier today," said Reuben. "Come on, tell us what it's all about. You don't have a big smile on your face for nothing."

"Well, Dan was right," smiled Simeon. "When God promises something, you just have to be patient. Just because he doesn't answer at once doesn't mean that he's forgotten."

"Forgotten what?" said Jacob impatiently.

"Now it's your turn to be patient," joked Simeon.

"Do stop teasing us," pleaded Dan. "It must be something to do with what we were talking about the other day."

Simeon couldn't keep the good news to himself a minute longer. As he told them what had happened in the Temple, their eyes grew wider and wider with amazement. And you know exactly what he told them, don't you?

* * *

Stimulus questions

1. What did Simeon tell Reuben, Dan and Jacob about?
2. What made Simeon very unhappy? What things make you unhappy?
3. Simeon had a group of friends to share his problems with. Why is it good to have friends to talk to? What sort of things can you talk to your friends about – good things and bad things?
4. Can you think of something that you have been promised that you had to wait a long time for? How did you feel?

Thinking time

1. Think of something that you have been able to share with your friends. If it was a happy thing, how did it make you feel? If it was a sad thing, how did it make you feel?
2. Think of something you were promised that you had to wait a long time for. How did you feel?

Prayer

"Lord, thank you for the friends we can share our happy and sad times with. Help us to wait patiently for promises to be kept. Amen."

PETER LOSES JEMMA

THEME: **Keeping Promises**
Breaking promises causes unhappiness.

"…and Peter," shouted Mrs Robinson, as he ran down the drive, "you will keep your promise and remember to collect Jemma after school, won't you?"

"I promise," Peter shouted back at his mother. "You can depend on me."

Jemma was only six. Her mother usually collected her from school, but on this particular day she was planning to visit her mother who had been ill, and wasn't sure that she would be back in time. Peter, being in Year 6 and feeling very grown-up, didn't much like the idea of walking home with Jemma, but on this occasion he agreed to help his mother. Anyway, he quite liked his little sister, but it didn't do to show this too openly.

When school finished, Peter remembered that he had to collect Jemma. As soon as Miss Dexter had dismissed the class, Jemma rushed out to meet Peter who, with a great sense of responsibility, said, "Jemma, have you got your coat and lunch box – and your reading book?"

"Of course I have, Peter," she replied impatiently. "I am six, you know!"

"All right, but I don't want to get home and find you've forgotten something," he added.

They were just about to go through the school gate when Peter was met by a group of his friends.

"Eh! Peter," John called, "what about a quick game of football before going home? We need the practice before the match on Saturday morning."

"Yes, OK," Peter replied quickly, but then he remembered he had Jemma with him. "Oh, I've forgotten, I've got to go straight home today. Sorry!"

"Not like you to miss the chance of a kick-about," remarked Clive.

"Just fancy, the team captain refusing to practise," jeered David.

This was too much for Peter. He took his responsibility as captain of the team very seriously and didn't like to think that his friends thought he was letting them down.

"OK then," he shouted back to them, "I'll see you on the field in five minutes."

"Jemma," Peter said to his sister, who had not been paying attention to his talk about football practice, "I've something important to do for about ten minutes. Will you go into the library and read your book for a little while?"

"But we're supposed to go straight home," she pleaded.

"I know, but Mum said she might not be home when we got back from school, so it won't matter if we're a bit late," he replied.

"All right," she agreed reluctantly, "but don't be longer than ten minutes."

Peter got her settled in the library and rushed off for his kick about with the others.

When Peter got involved in football, time seemed to have little meaning, and his ten minutes became 20 and then half an hour. Jemma had read her next chapter and was wondering where Peter was, when who should pop his head round the library door but Mr Wheeler, the head teacher.

"Hello, Jemma," he said, "what are you still doing here at this time? Hasn't your mother come?"

"Mummy's gone to see Grandma and didn't think she

would be back in time to pick me up, so Peter's supposed to be taking me home," Jemma explained.

"Well, where is he, then?" enquired Mr Wheeler.

"He left me here and said he had something very important to do and that he'd be back in ten minutes. But that was ages ago," she said rather tearfully.

"Don't you worry," said Mr Wheeler cheerily, "I'll go and see if I can find him."

He searched the corridors and the classrooms but, of course, he could not find Peter.

"I don't know what's happened to Peter," he said to Jemma, "but don't worry, I'll ring your home just to see if your Mum has arrived back, and if there's someone in I'll run you home in my car."

He was back in less than two minutes. "It's all right, Jemma," he said, "your Mum's got back from Grandma's. I told her that I would take you home in my car."

A few minutes later Peter rushed into the library, quite out of breath, and without looking round for Jemma, said, "Sorry I've been so long, Jemma. I hope you've been OK." But there was no reply, and a thorough search of the library produced no Jemma either! "Oh dear," muttered Peter under his breath, "where has she gone? The last thing I told her was to stay here till I came. I'm in trouble now. I can't go home without her!" He set about doing a complete search of the school, but by this time the place was deserted. There was nothing else he could do but to go home. He was turning all sorts of things over in his mind – what would his mother and father say if he turned up without her? What if she's decided to go to a friend's house on the way home? What if she's got lost? What if she's been kidnapped? Things got worse and worse. He eventually turned into his drive to be met by his mother, who said angrily, "And where's Jemma, do you suppose?"

"I...I...I...don't know," he spluttered, with a lump rising in his throat. "She wasn't in the library where I left her."

"Well, young man, thanks to Mr Wheeler, she's at home safe and sound," his mother snapped. "But no thanks to you, Peter!"

"I'm sorry, Mum," he said feebly. "I hope she's all right."

"You promised me faithfully that you would collect her and bring her straight home. Why can't you do a simple thing like that? When you make a promise, you've got to keep it. If we can't trust you to keep promises about little things, how can we trust you with anything? You'd better go inside and get washed for tea – you look as if you've been rolling in a mud bath. I've a good idea what you've been doing!" Mrs Robinson was so angry, but relieved that Jemma was home safely. Peter felt about as miserable as he had ever felt in all his life. He'd let Jemma down, his mother and father, his head teacher, who was bound to know what had happened, but most of all, he felt he had let himself down.

It was only later that evening, when Jemma had gone to bed, that Peter went into the lounge and plucked up courage to speak to his parents. "I really am sorry for what I did," he whispered just loud enough for them to hear. "I've let everyone down. I'm so glad Jemma's all right." Mr and Mrs Robinson had calmed down by now, and the three of them had a long chat about what exactly had happened. "I've learned my lesson," Peter finally said. "A promise is a promise!"

* * *

Stimulus questions

1. What should Peter have done when his friends asked him to play football?
2. How did Jemma feel waiting in the library? And Peter when she wasn't there? And her Mum?

3. What sort of promises do you sometimes make? Think of a promise you didn't keep. Why not?

Thinking time

1. Think of a time that you didn't keep a promise. How did you feel? How did other people feel?

Prayer

"Lord, when we make promises, give us strength to keep them. Forgive us when we fail, and give us courage to say we are sorry to those we have hurt. Amen."

JESUS VISITS THE TEMPLE AS A BOY
LUKE 2:41-52

THEME: **Growing Up**

Growing up brings all sorts of surprises and worries for parents.

"We must be making plans for our annual visit to Jerusalem," Joseph said to Mary as he put another log on the fire. "We've been to the Passover festival every year since we've been married. It's the most important of all our festivals – we ought to try to go again this year."

"Yes," agreed Mary, "we have such a good time meeting with all our friends and joining in all the activities at the Temple. We shall have to ask Elizabeth and Zechariah if Jesus can stay with them again while we're away," added Mary.

"Well, I've been thinking," said Joseph slowly. "Do you think we should take Jesus with us this year – he is twelve? It's the age that our faith thinks of boys as growing up to be adults."

"But it's such a long way, Joseph, and he's only twelve. Perhaps next year," said Mary.

"Well," said Joseph, "he's got to learn to grow up some time. He's very sensible – I'm sure he wouldn't be any trouble."

"I know," said Mary finally, "why don't we ask him tomorrow?"

Next morning, when they had finished their breakfast of bread and olives, Joseph managed to catch Jesus before he dashed off to meet his friends.

"Your mother and I have been thinking," Joseph said cautiously. "You know that we go to Jerusalem for the Passover festival each year, and you stay with Elizabeth and Zechariah – well, we wondered if you would like to come with us this year."

"Yes, I would," Jesus exclaimed. "That would be great. I've always wanted to go to Jerusalem – and some of my friends have already been. They say it's an enormous city with a huge Temple, bigger than anything in Nazareth."

"I thought you might like the idea," smiled Joseph, "but there are going to be crowds of people and it's a long journey. Once we've started there's no turning back."

"Don't worry, I am twelve," Jesus reminded Joseph.

The day finally came when Joseph, Mary and Jesus joined the rest of the people from Nazareth who were going to Jerusalem. It took several days to get there and Jesus found it quite hard work. When he got the first glimpse of Jerusalem, with the enormous Temple clearly visible on the horizon, he stood gazing at it in complete silence. Lots of thoughts were rushing through his head – some happy, some strangely sad and some that he couldn't understand at all.

The following day they went to the Temple itself. Joseph pointed out the main parts – the Court of the Gentiles, the Court of Israel, where only adult Jews could go, and the Holy of Holies where only the priests could go. Jesus felt very grown up being able to join Joseph in all the things that only adult Jews could do. What impressed him most were not the buildings, though they were beautiful, but the groups of people sitting around their teachers, discussing and asking questions.

"It was certainly a good idea to bring him with us," said Joseph. "I've never seen anyone so keen to listen to the teachers. Once or twice I thought he was going to join in, but he seemed a bit shy."

"I should think so," argued Mary. "He's only twelve, remember!"

The last day of the festival came and they had to think about setting off for home. Their group was all ready for the long trek back to Nazareth. When they camped at the end of the first day, Mary said to Joseph, "Have you seen Jesus anywhere?"

"Can't say I have," replied Joseph casually. "Come to that I don't think I've seen him all day. He'll come when he's hungry!"

"I do hope you're right," said Mary anxiously. "He is only twelve."

"Oh, don't worry," said Joseph, "he'll be with his friends – he's met such a lot of new people – quite the young man!" But Jesus did not turn up for supper that night.

"That's strange," said Joseph, "I felt sure he'd be here when it got dark. He's never done anything like this before."

"I'm worried," said Mary. "He's only twelve. He could easily get lost in all these crowds."

"We shall just have to leave our group and go back to Jerusalem," sighed Joseph.

"But he knew the festival was finished," argued Mary. "Why has he done this to us? The first time we really treat him as an adult, he behaves like a child and gets lost!" Mary could not contain her tears of worry, which were mingled with anger.

"I know," said Joseph, trying to comfort Mary, "but I feel sure he'll be all right."

Well, they searched and searched. They went to all the places in Jerusalem they had visited, but there was no sign of him. No one had seen a boy of twelve fitting Jesus' description. They searched for three days without any success. They were just about to report him missing to the authorities, when Mary said, "You don't think that he could still be in the Temple, do you, Joseph? You said how interested he was in all that was happening."

"But the festival is finished. What could he be doing there? But it's worth a try – we've looked everywhere else," sighed Joseph.

They searched the Temple thoroughly, and were just about

to give up, when Joseph noticed a group of people in a corner sitting round a teacher. As Mary and Joseph got nearer, they saw the unmistakable face of Jesus. He was not only listening, but also joining in the discussion and asking questions! The older men seemed very impressed with what he had to say. Mary and Joseph were stunned. They looked at each other in amazement, but said nothing. It was Mary who couldn't contain herself a moment longer. "Jesus, why have you treated us like this? Your father and I have been anxiously searching for you." Jesus looked puzzled. "Searching for me?" he said. "Didn't you realise that I had to be in my Father's house?" Mary looked at Joseph; Joseph looked at Mary; and they both looked at Jesus. They didn't know what to think. They certainly didn't understand what Jesus meant.

As they made their way home, Mary and Joseph talked and talked about what had happened. "One thing is sure," said Joseph, "he's not a child any more." Mary had to agree. There were so many things about Jesus she did not fully understand, but she kept them in her mind. Perhaps one day everything would become clear.

* * *

Stimulus questions

1. What might Joseph and Mary have said to each other when they couldn't find Jesus?
2. What did Joseph and Mary learn about Jesus from this incident?
3. Can you think of things that you were allowed to do for the first time?
4. Can you think of things that you were not allowed to do because your parents thought you were too young? Do you think they were right?

Thinking time

1. Think of a time when you were trusted to do something for the very first time. How did you feel?
2. Think of a time when things went wrong because you did not behave sensibly. How did you feel?

Prayer

"Lord, we thank you for all the new things we can do as we grow up. Forgive us when things go wrong and cause our parents to worry about us. Help us to learn to do better next time. Amen."

"THEY'RE NOT CHILDREN ANY MORE!"

THEME: **Growing Up**

Growing up is not easy for children or for their parents.

The Robinson family had spent their summer holidays for the past few years in a caravan in Devon. In fact, Peter, who was ten (nearly eleven, as he kept on reminding everyone), and Sarah, aged eight, couldn't remember a time when they hadn't gone to the caravan for two weeks in August. They really did enjoy it, but after so many years going to the same place, they were getting rather bored with doing the same things every year. It was all right for their little sister Jemma. She was only six and was still quite happy to go to the same place and do the same things – which for her meant bucket and spade on the beach and plenty of ice-creams! It was when they were finishing tea one Friday after school, that the question of summer holidays arose.

"Only two more weeks and it'll be the end of term," Mrs Robinson said half-heartedly. She knew that the children looked forward to the long holidays, but six weeks was a long time to have three boisterous children at home.

"Only two weeks?" said Mr Robinson with surprise. "We shall have to think about where we're going for our holidays this year."

"Don't tell me," butted in Peter rather cheekily, "let me guess. Could it be to the caravan in Devon by any chance?"

"How did you know we were going there?" asked Jemma innocently.

"Because that's where we've been for the last 150 years!" replied Sarah with a note of scorn in her voice.

"Well, I like it there," insisted Jemma.

"You would," cried Peter. "You've not been going there as many times as we have!"

"Now then," said Mr Robinson firmly, "there's no need to get so worked up about it. Anyway, who said we were going to the caravan again? I think we'd better let the subject drop before we all get really angry."

So that was that. No one said another word about holidays, though Peter reckoned it would be the caravan again – and Sarah agreed with him. Later that evening, when the three children were finally in bed, Steve and Kate Robinson looked at each other but said nothing for a long time. Then Kate broke the silence.

"That was quite an outburst at tea tonight! I've never known Peter and Sarah behave like that – and about going away on holiday as well. They sounded very ungrateful. We always try to give them a good time when we go to Devon – and they get extra pocket money!"

"Yes, they really told us what they thought about going to the caravan again," Steve added. "Only Jemma seemed to want to go. I guess it's a sign that Peter and Sarah are beginning to grow up, though I think Sarah would be all right if it wasn't for Peter giving her ideas."

"Perhaps they have a point," said Kate. "We do take it for granted that they will want to go to Devon again – we never think of asking them for their ideas."

"I expect you're right," agreed Steve. "They may still be children but they are growing up. It won't be long before Jemma is joining them and then what chance shall we have against the three of them!"

"Let's really surprise them," Kate said with a glint in her eye. "Mrs Jackson told me only this morning that they had booked a self-catering chalet in Majorca big enough for eight and she wondered if we would like to go with them. Our three get on so well with their Paul – and we would be able to share the cooking and washing-up. What do you think, Steve?"

"That sounds a great idea, Kate," Steve agreed. "I'll book flights and get some euros. We've got passports, so it should be quite easy. Let's keep it a big surprise."

So it was all arranged. After tea, a few days before they were due to fly to Majorca, Mr Robinson said in a pretend stern voice, "Mum and I have definitely decided that we are not going to Devon in a caravan this year." The children looked a little anxious and Jemma's bottom lip began to quiver. "We listened to all that Peter and Sarah had to say, and we've decided to go somewhere else for a surprise."

"Wow," said Peter, "you don't mean we're going to *Cornwall* in a caravan instead!"

"Now that's enough of that, young man," snapped Mr Robinson. "If you go into the lounge and use your brains, I think you'll soon discover where we're going."

The three children rushed excitedly into the lounge. There on the coffee table were three flight bags and three plastic packets with some euros inside. Peter and Sarah looked at each other speechlessly, but Jemma picked up one of the plastic packets and took out the notes. She looked at them suspiciously before saying, "100 *'heroes'* – this isn't real money!"

"Oh yes it is," butted in Peter, "and it's *euros*, not *'heroes'*!"

"That means we're going to Spain or Italy or somewhere else where they use euros," added Sarah, "and that explains these flight bags."

They were so excited they could hardly stop chattering. Jemma joined in, though she didn't really seem to know what all the fuss was about.

"But just a minute," shouted Mr Robinson above the din, "perhaps you don't think it's such a good idea. We didn't ask you about it first – you may think it's a rubbish idea."

"That's all right, Dad," said Peter with a twinkle in his eye, "it's a great surprise – but you might like to ask us for our ideas next year!"

* * *

Stimulus questions

1. When Peter and Sarah grumbled about going to Devon in a caravan again, Mrs Robinson said that they seemed ungrateful. Do you think they were? Were they really being rude?
2. Do you think their parents should have discussed going to Spain with the children before making the arrangements? Why?
3. What sort of things do you wish your parents would discuss with you?
4. How can you let your parents know that you are "growing up" and would like to be asked about things without seeming to be ungrateful or rude to them?
5. Why is it hard for parents to learn that you are "growing up"? Why is it hard for you?

Thinking time

1. Think of a time when you quarrelled at home about something you wanted to do. How did you feel?
2. Think of how you might have behaved to avoid the quarrel.

Prayer

"Lord, growing up isn't easy for children or their parents. When our parents trust us with something, help us to behave sensibly, so that they will learn to trust us more. Amen."

JOHN THE BAPTIST'S COURAGE
LUKE 3:1-18

THEME: **Courage**
It often takes great courage to say and do what is right. It would be easier to say and do nothing.

John, the son of Zechariah and Elizabeth, was about six months older than Jesus. They were cousins. Very unusual things happened when John was born, not least that he was called John. The first boy to be born into a family was almost always named after his father or grandfather. But Zechariah had been most insistent that their boy would be called John. That's the name that God told him to give the baby.

What's more, God had a special job for John to do. His special work was to prepare people for when Jesus came teaching and healing. It was difficult, in the days before radio, television, newspapers, telephones and the internet, to let lots of people know what was going to happen. You just had to have someone to go round shouting it out and hoping that people would listen and take notice. That's what John had to do. What he had to tell the people was not very pleasant. If they were to be ready for when Jesus came, they had to put a lot of things right in their own lives. Reminding them of this took a great deal of courage. It wasn't easy to point out people's faults, especially as John knew that he wasn't that good himself. It would have been a lot easier for John to have said "No" and gone off to be a fisherman or a carpenter!

So, when he was about 30, John went into the desert, where it was quiet and away from all the crowds, to think about how he should set about his important job. He knew that it was no good just reminding people of their faults – he also had to do something to help them. Those who realised their faults and wanted to be forgiven, he could wash in water. He could take them to a river and pour water over their heads to show that just as you can use water to wash something clean, so God is able to clean up a person's life.

So with great fear and trepidation he made a start! He didn't go to the big towns, but stayed in the desert where there were only a few people. Perhaps he was a bit scared to go where there were lots of people – who knows what they might do to him? However, word soon got round about this prophet in the desert and crowds of people, of all kinds, went out to hear what he had to say. He took a great risk in what he said.

"You're just like snakes," he shouted, "trying to wriggle away from trouble! It's no good trying to hide from God – you've got to start living decent lives – being kind and just and fair to people. And it's no good saying that your great, great, great, great grandfather was Abraham. It's what *you* are like that matters!"

Well, that was giving it to them straight. He waited, his stomach churning inside, wondering what they would do. He must have pricked their consciences, because they all fell quiet and looked down with shame. They knew he was right. After a while, one of them said, "What can we do to put things right?"

"It's like this," said John more calmly. "If you've got two coats, give one of them to someone who hasn't got one – and the same with your food." That was easy for them to understand, but not so easy to do.

Among the crowd were some tax collectors. Now they were not very popular with anyone. It wasn't that they made people pay tax (that's only fair if they wanted the government to build roads and bridges, for example), but they overcharged and put the extra money in their own pockets. They blushed with shame when John said, "Don't charge more than you have to!"

Some soldiers had turned up just in case there was any trouble. "What about us then?" they asked John, wondering if he would dare to criticise them.

"Don't bully people just because you are soldiers, and don't arrest people just because they can't afford to pay you a bribe! And while we're talking of money, be satisfied with your pay!" The crowds were hushed into silence. No one had ever dared to speak to soldiers like that. But they took the point and agreed that he was right.

Lots of people changed their lives and were baptised as a sign that they wanted to start a new life. So there were many that were ready and keen to hear what Jesus had to say when he started his work of preaching, teaching and healing.

John had faithfully done the job that God had given him to do, though it took great courage and there must have been times when it would have been easy to give it all up and go and get an ordinary job somewhere. It didn't end happily for John, either. When he pointed out some great fault in the life of one of the rulers, he was thrown in jail and finally put to death.

* * *

Stimulus questions

1. What sorts of jobs require great courage? Why do people choose to do dangerous jobs?
2. Why did the work that God wanted John to do require great courage?
3. What did he call the people? Why? What were the tax collectors doing that was wrong? What did he tell them to do? How did the soldiers behave towards people? What did John have to say to them?
4. Did the people take any notice of him? What did John do to help people show that they were really sorry for what they had done, and wanted to start a new life?
5. Can you think of something you had to do that needed courage? What did you do?

Thinking time

1. Think of a time when you had to do something that needed courage. How did you feel? What helped you to do it?

Prayer

"Lord, thank you for all those who do dangerous jobs. When we have to do things that are difficult, give us courage to do what is right. Amen."

CAROLINE'S GREAT COURAGE

THEME: **Courage**

Sometimes we are called upon to show real courage.

"Mum," piped up Jemma as she was walking home after school with Mrs Robinson, "how old do you have to be to drive a coach?"

"I'm not exactly sure," replied her mother, "but I know you have to be older to drive a coach than a car, and you can't begin to learn to drive a car until you are seventeen. Why do you ask, dear? Have you decided you want to be a coach driver when you grow up?"

"No, silly," replied Jemma. "Anyway I'm only six. I would have to wait ages."

That seemed to be the end of that conversation, until they turned into their road, and Jemma said proudly, "Well, I know someone who drove a coach and she was only thirteen."

"Whoever told you that?" Mrs Robinson said rather scornfully.

"We were told in assembly this morning. It was a girl called Caroline, who used to go to our school, and she was very courageous."

"It sounds a very dangerous thing to do to me. I expect she got into trouble for it, and serves her right too. Don't you get any ideas into your head, young lady!" And with that the conversation really did come to an end.

At teatime Peter said he had some very important news for his Mum and Dad.

"We heard about it in assembly this morning," butted in Sarah.

"I've already tried to tell Mum," blurted out little Jemma, "and I got told off for it!"

"I should think so," insisted her mother. "Girls of thirteen have no right to be driving coaches!"

"But you've got it all wrong, Mum," moaned Peter. "What Caroline did probably saved everyone's life."

"And Caroline's going to be at next Friday's assembly to get a police bravery award. All the parents are invited – will you come, Mum?"

"I think I must have got things a little confused. I'll try to come on Friday; I usually do come to the parents' assemblies."

Next Friday the hall was packed full with children and parents. There was quite a lot of chattering going on, but as soon as the quiet music played, a hush descended. Mr Wheeler, the head teacher, walked to the front, followed by an older girl and then a very tall policeman in uniform with lots of silver buttons.

"Good morning, everyone," said Mr Wheeler. "Today is a very special day. Those of you who have been at King's Road School for some years will know that this is Caroline Thompson. She has come back to see you all for a special purpose and I am going to ask Chief Inspector Price to tell you why."

"Good morning," said the Chief Inspector, clearing his throat, "I am here to present Caroline with a police bravery award for an act of outstanding courage. Caroline was coming home on the school bus, when unfortunately the driver became ill and collapsed at the wheel. But I'm sure you'd like Caroline to tell her own story." With that he sat down and smiled at Caroline. She nervously got to her feet and began her story.

"Well, it wasn't anything really," she said in a tiny voice. "When the driver collapsed, the coach swerved across the road towards the oncoming traffic. Everyone screamed with panic and ducked down behind the seats. I was sitting near the front, and just thought that something had to be done to try to stop a nasty accident. I don't know what made me do it, but I made a grab for the steering wheel and tried to get the coach on the correct side of the road. I've never driven anything in my life, except dodgem cars – but this was no fun fair! Eventually the coach got on the right side, but I didn't know what to do to stop it – the driver was still in his seat and I didn't know which pedal was the brake. Luckily, we started to go uphill which slowed the coach down."

"How did the coach finally stop?" asked the Chief Inspector.

"When we hit a lamp post!" grinned Caroline. "I jumped out and waved at a passing car and asked the driver to call for help on his mobile phone."

"You must have been frightened," said Chief Inspector Price.

"I wasn't really scared," Caroline replied. "I didn't have time to think about that – but we were all a bit shaken up afterwards. My friends thought I'd done a really good job, but I'm surprised that I'm getting an award. I didn't think I'd done that much really." With that she sat down looking quite shy.

Everyone in the hall clapped loudly as Chief Inspector Price presented Caroline with her bravery award. "Caroline's lightning reactions certainly prevented a more serious accident, and she showed outstanding courage," he added.

As Jemma and her Mum walked home from school that afternoon, Mrs Robinson said, "Jemma, I'm very sorry that I was cross with you when you first told me about Caroline driving a coach. I realise now that she was a very brave girl."

"That's all right, Mum," Jemma said chirpily, "I think I might like to be a coach driver when I grow up after all."

* * *

Stimulus questions

1. Who are some of the special visitors that come to our assemblies? Why do you think we invite them to come?
2. When Caroline told what she did, why did she say, "It wasn't anything, really"?
3. Do you think that what she did was because she knew she would get a special bravery award?
4. Being a coach driver is a very responsible job. How should we behave on school buses to make things easier for the driver?
5. Have you been in a situation when you or someone else acted with great courage?

Thinking time

1. Think of when you go on coaches for school outings. Think of the things you can do to make the driver's job easier.

Prayer

"Lord, we thank you for coach drivers who bring us to school and take us on outings. Help us to do all we can to make their job easier, so that we have safe journeys. Amen."

JESUS IS TEMPTED
LUKE 4:1-13

THEME: **Temptation**

Being tempted is not wrong; giving in to it is.

For many years Jesus had a growing feeling that he had a very special job to do for God. Ever since that visit to the Temple in Jerusalem when he was twelve, he knew that he had a special link with God. All people were children of God, but he felt that he was the Son of God. What convinced him was the voice he heard when he was baptised by John: "You are my Son," it said, loud and clear. It was not something that he could easily talk about to other people – they would soon put him in his place, telling him not to be bigheaded. But it wasn't that he felt that he was somebody great – in fact, the opposite was true. He felt that real greatness was about serving and helping other people. He had a deep-down feeling that God was asking him to show people what God was like, by serving and helping them. The question was, how?

He was about 30 when these feelings grew very strong and so he went out into the desert to think and pray quietly. He spent nearly six weeks there, all alone, with very little to eat. After such a long time he was very hungry.

It was just then that he seemed to hear a voice.

"If you are the Son of God, why be hungry? Tell these stones to become freshly baked crusty loaves of bread." The thought of freshly baked bread made his mouth water!

"What harm would there be in doing that?" he thought. "If I am the Son of God, better to try it out here where there is no one to see if nothing happens! And if I could do this for myself, then I could go round doing it for all the hungry people – and there are plenty of them. That way they would listen to me and what I had to say about God."

It all seemed too good to be true. But Jesus remembered a verse from the Jewish law that said, "People do not live just on bread." God wanted him to be more than someone to fill people's stomachs. Having fed them once they'd be hungry again the next day. He wanted to give them something that lasted for ever. So Jesus put that idea right out of his mind.

Another day, when he was dozing in the hot midday sun, he had a sort of dream in which he was on a high mountain looking down on all the countries of the world. Again that same evil voice whispered to him, "With all your power you could become the leader of the whole world and then people would listen to your message. You would have to accept all the evil in the world, but it would be worth it, wouldn't it?"

Jesus thought hard. He knew that kings and emperors only got their power by wars in which many people suffered. This couldn't be right. He remembered the first commandment that he had learned as a child, "You shall worship the Lord your God and serve him only." How could he show people that God was a God of love and peace by doing things that brought suffering and sadness? That's not God's way. He put the idea right out of his head.

Some time later he had another dream in which he saw himself standing on the highest point of the Temple in Jerusalem, where he could see below all the people worshipping God. There were hundreds of people scurrying about like tiny ants. That same voice of evil said to him, "Why don't you jump down into the crowds? They'll be amazed when they see you leap. There's no need to worry about hurting yourself, because one of great King David's psalms says that God will send his angels to protect his chosen servant."

"Now that would impress people," Jesus thought, "and

what it says about God's angels saving me is in the Scriptures. Wouldn't everyone know for certain that I was sent by God?"

But it didn't seem right to him. Why should he deliberately do something stupid, like jumping from the top of the Temple, and then expect God to save him? Having seen this daredevil jump, the people would expect something even more daring next time.

"I can't keep testing God out," Jesus concluded. "He sent me to serve other people and if necessary to suffer for them. This is the way that people will really come to know God."

Jesus put these temptations right out of his mind as he began his work of teaching and healing, but it wasn't the last time that the voice of evil tried to turn him away from what he knew was right.

* * *

Stimulus questions

1. When Jesus visited the Temple when he was twelve, he knew he had a special job to do for God. Can you remember that story? (Luke 2:41–52)
2. Jesus thought that people who were really "great" were those who helped others. Is that what people today think being "great" is? Who are some of the really great people today?
3. Jesus went into the desert to think quietly. Do you have a special place where you like to go to think things out? Where is it?
4. Why didn't Jesus turn the stones into loaves of bread?
5. Why didn't Jesus try to become a great conquering king?
6. Why didn't Jesus jump from the Temple?
7. Can you think of a time when you were tempted to do something you knew was wrong?

Thinking time

1. Think of Jesus in the desert, feeling very hungry and not having much food. Think how he might feel when he could smell fresh, hot, crusty loaves of bread. Think how hard it was for him not to change the stones into bread.

2. Think of a time when you were tempted to do something wrong. How did you feel? Did you do it, or did you find courage to say "No!"?

Prayer

"Lord, forgive us for the times we have done or said things that were wrong or hurtful to others. When we are tempted again, give us courage to say and do what is right. Amen."

PETER IS TEMPTED

THEME: **Temptation**
It is often very hard to do what is right.

There were two things on Peter's mind as he walked home from school. One was the Inter-school Football Final next week. Peter was captain of King's Road Primary football team. The other thing on his mind was his Dad's birthday in two weeks' time. His problem here was money for a present.

He was just crossing the road when he noticed a group of four or five other boys on the other side. They all went to Green Park Primary, the school they were playing in the football final.

"Hey," shouted the biggest of the group, "aren't you the kid who goes to King's Road, and aren't you the captain of that useless football team?"

"What if I am?" replied Peter defensively.

"Well, we've got a deal to make with you that could make you £5 richer," said another.

"What sort of deal?" asked Peter suspiciously.

"Well, it's like this. Our team reckons that you score at least one goal every match. The deal is this – we give you £5 if you guarantee not to score any goals in the final next week."

"That's bribery. Football matches are about the best team winning," replied Peter.

"OK, if that's how you want it," said the first big boy, "but it's an easy way to earn £5."

Peter thought rapidly. He wasn't rich and he did need some money for his Dad's birthday present pretty fast. £5 for doing nothing? It was only a game anyway.

"Come on then," the gang shouted impatiently, "what do you say?"

"W…w…well, OK then," muttered Peter.

"See you next week at the match," they all jeered. "No need for you to bother to practise!"

Peter felt bad – very bad. He'd never been involved in anything like this. He argued with himself one way and then the other. He knew it couldn't be right to accept a bribe; he knew that the rest of the team were expecting him to play well; he wouldn't just be letting himself down, but the rest of the team and the whole school. But on the other hand, it was a quick solution to the problem of his Dad's birthday present.

Though he didn't say anything about this to his parents, they knew something was wrong.

"What's the matter with you, Peter?" grumbled his mother. "When you get up in a morning you look as if you haven't had a wink of sleep all night; and you poke around with your food as if I'm trying to poison you." "Nothing's the matter," was all they could get out of him.

The day of the final arrived. While the rest of the team were excited and confident, Peter wearily changed into his football kit and with his shoulders drooping and head hanging low he shuffled out onto the pitch. He felt terrible. The sight of the gang from Green Park on the touchline didn't help, especially when one of them waved a £5 note in the air.

Play was fairly evenly balanced until five minutes before half-time. Peter had been letting good passes to him in front of the goalmouth just go straight past. He felt sure they could have been two goals up by now. Instead, in a wild flurry of activity Green Park scored and then a minute before the whistle they were given a penalty, from which they scored. During half-time, the King's Road team just didn't know what to think. They didn't like saying anything, but they couldn't help noticing that Peter just wasn't playing his usual game. It wasn't like him to miss passes and to shoot wide at an open goal. Peter, for his part, was feeling terrible. He did some rapid thinking. What had happened to him to get into this position? He had always enjoyed sport and now he hated every minute of it. He had always stood up for what was right, so why had he given in this time? It was important to get his Dad something for his birthday, but it needn't cost a lot – he was always being reminded that it was the thought that counts, so why had he given in to the temptation to get an easy £5? He'd been fooled into throwing away all that he really cared about. Well, he thought to himself, the game's not lost yet!

"Come on, lads," he shouted as they started the second half, "we can do it yet!"

Peter played with a new confidence. He seemed to be just in the right place when a pass came his way and, with perfect timing and careful control, he shot the ball into the corner of the net. The team were delighted – this was the Peter they knew. Ten minutes later King's Road were given a corner. The right winger who took the corner lifted it high into the centre and though the goalkeeper seemed to have it covered, Peter jumped higher than the keeper's outstretched arm and glanced the ball into the net. The team went wild with excitement – 2–2, and five minutes left to play. David Parkin, who played outside Peter, passed him the ball, and with 20 metres to the goalmouth, Peter dribbled the ball forward. He beat three players and got himself into the penalty area. He was about to shoot, when an opposing defender made a flying tackle that took Peter's feet from under him, leaving the ball to trickle forward. The referee had no hesitation in awarding a penalty. Peter was the obvious person to take the kick. He was a bit shaken from the harsh tackle, but got to his feet and settled the ball on the spot. This was the big one. Not only would it win the match and the cup final, thought Peter, it would be a goal for what was right. Peter calmed himself, and took a few deep breaths before the few steps to the ball. Just before he kicked, he noticed the goalkeeper move his body to the left, so Peter adjusted his kick and without any great force placed it in the right hand corner. The noise that erupted was deafening and they managed to hold on to their lead until the final whistle. They had won 3–2!

King's Road had won the Inter-school Cup Final – the first time for six years! As Peter celebrated with the rest of the team, he couldn't help thinking how proud he felt to have scored a hat-trick in the final. When they had all calmed down and were getting changed, Peter had no doubt in his mind that the thing he felt best about was that he had beaten off the temptation to take the easy way. He never heard any more from the Green Park gang and a bit of extra work at the weekend, cleaning neighbours' cars, soon earned enough for a decent birthday present for his Dad.

* * *

Stimulus questions

1. When Peter was feeling bad about promising not to score a goal, what could he have done? Should he have told his teacher or his parents, or discussed it with his friends?
2. During half-time, was he right to change his mind about not scoring? Why?

Thinking time

1. Think how Peter felt when he promised not to score.
2. Think of a time when you felt bad about something you promised to do that you knew was wrong. What could you have done instead?

Prayer

"Lord, forgive us when we do and say things which are wrong because this seems the easy way out of trouble. Give us courage to say and do what is right, even when it is hard. Amen."

JESUS IS REJECTED BY HIS OWN PEOPLE
LUKE 4:14-30

THEME: **Bullying**

Sometimes people who know us are jealous of our achievements and reject and bully us.

Jesus spent about six weeks in the desert trying to work out just how he was going to serve God. He finally decided that the best way to show people what God was really like and how he wanted them to behave, was not by bossing them around, but by helping them.

Having got this clear in his mind, he returned to Nazareth, the town where he was brought up and where he was well known. At least he would have some friends among the people who came to hear him teach. On the Jews' special day, called the Sabbath, he went to the synagogue to worship God his Father as he did every week. They invited him to read from the Scriptures, and the part for that Sabbath was from the prophet Isaiah.

In a loud, clear voice Jesus read, "The Spirit of the Lord is on me to preach good news to the poor. God has sent me to seek freedom for prisoners, to give the blind their sight back and give people in trouble some real hope for the future."

Now Isaiah was speaking of the one that God would send to be the people's Saviour, but of course, *this* Saviour was Jesus himself! So Jesus looked up at the people, took a deep breath and said slowly and calmly, "What Isaiah is talking about is happening before your very eyes – I am the one he is speaking about."

There was a deathly silence in the synagogue and every eye was fixed on Jesus. They had never heard anyone speak like this before. They were used to hearing Isaiah tell about the coming Saviour, but they never thought anyone would stand up and say, "This Saviour is me!"

After a while, quiet muttering broke out among the people.

"I've heard that Jesus has done some wonderful things," said one.

"Yes," added another, "they say he has healed people in Capernaum."

"He's not done anything here in Nazareth," objected one. "Perhaps these stories are just rumours."

"Not much good if he can't do a few miracles in his home city of Nazareth," commented another.

"Anyway, who does he think he is," added an old man, "saying that he is the Saviour that Isaiah said would come?"

"That sounds a load of rubbish to me," grumbled an old woman. "We know who he is; he's the son of Joseph the carpenter!"

"Doesn't take much for some people to get big ideas about themselves," muttered a few others.

"How can he be the Saviour, when we know his parents are ordinary villagers? Whoever could imagine that God's Saviour would be the son of a carpenter?"

This was the conclusion most of the crowd came to.

Jesus then shouted above the noise, "I expect you want me to prove who I am by doing some of the miracles I did in Capernaum."

"That's right," they all shouted back, "let's see some miracles – perhaps that'll show who you really are – Saviour, indeed!"

"I'll tell you the truth," Jesus continued. "It's hard for anyone to be accepted in his home town. All the prophets that God has sent have been rejected by their own people. Often the prophets did more good for people who were not Jews at all."

The people were furious when they heard this. They thought that they were God's favourites. Here was this man they had known from being a boy, the son of a village carpenter, claiming that people had rejected the prophets God had sent and yet saying that he was God's Saviour!

What Jesus had said was quite true, but the people didn't like to hear the truth. They were full of jealousy. They got up, grabbed hold of Jesus, and marched him out of town to the edge of a cliff.

"We'll teach him a lesson he won't forget in a long time," they jeered.

"We'll soon knock out of his head this silly idea of being the Saviour," they taunted.

Grabbing Jesus by the arms, they pulled him to the very edge of the cliff, as if to throw him over. Then, shaking them loose, Jesus stared hard at them and, calmly walking through the crowd, he went on his way. He couldn't help thinking that this was not a very promising start to his work, but it did show him that trying to help people was not going to be easy.

*   *   *

Stimulus questions

1. Why were the people so angry with Jesus?
2. Why did they think he was making it up about being God's Saviour? (carpenter's son)
3. Was Jesus really boasting about how great he was? How can you tell? (wanted to serve)
4. Why did they march him to the edge of the cliff? How do you think he felt?
5. Can you think of a time when other people left you out of things or laughed at you? How did you feel? How did you react?

Thinking time

1. Think of a time when other people left you out of things or laughed at you. How did they treat you? How did you feel?

Prayer

"Lord, sometimes people are unkind to us by not wanting to play with us or by laughing at us. Give us courage not to be afraid and to help them understand us better. Amen."

PETER IS BULLIED BY "HIS FRIENDS"

THEME: **Bullying**

Jealousy can lead to rejection and bullying.

When Peter Robinson was in Year 6, he became captain of King's Road School's football team. His greatest ambition was for King's Road to win the Inter-school Football Trophy. You can imagine the excitement when they got into the final against Green Park School. King's Road were 2–0 down at half-time, but then made a brilliant recovery. Peter scored two goals to level the match at 2–2 with just five minutes left to play. In the dying moments of the game King's Road were awarded a penalty for a nasty foul on Peter and he managed to slot his kick into the corner of the net. The King's Road supporters went wild with excitement and Peter was pleased to have scored a hat-trick, though he was the first to admit that it was a team effort.

The cup was presented to Peter, as captain, at a Friday assembly when parents were invited. Peter's Dad managed to get some time off work to come with Mrs Robinson. They were so proud when Peter was presented with the cup (especially when he remembered to say "thank you"). Everybody in the hall cheered the team loudly. Well, not quite everybody. There were three or four Year 6s who, instead of clapping enthusiastically, were doing a slow hand clap. Peter noticed this and wondered what it meant. As they came out of assembly, he soon found out.

"You won't be able to get into the classroom, Robinson," one of them sneered.

"Why not?" questioned Peter.

"'Cos the door won't be wide enough to get your head through!" came the reply, and they rolled about with laughter. Peter didn't know what to say – he just smiled faintly and walked on.

Peter had never come across this attitude before and didn't know what to do. He was generally very popular and never boasted about his football achievements. Things got worse. When they were having a kick-about in the playground before school one morning, one of this group quite deliberately kicked the ball at Peter at very close range. It hit him hard on the side of the face. When he turned to see who had kicked, all he heard was, "S-o-r-r-y, it should have gone in goal", with more of the same sneering laughter. Walking down the corridor later that morning, Peter saw this small group coming the other way. As they passed, one of them barged into him, knocking him into the wall. "Foul, Ref. Penalty!" the others jeered, and ran on.

This was too much. Peter didn't know what to do. He knew that bullying wasn't allowed and would be treated very seriously. Should he tell his class teacher? He wasn't really sure whether this was bullying, but it was certainly making him feel very unhappy.

Peter's Mum and Dad noticed that something wasn't quite right. For a few days Peter had been looking rather miserable.

"Come on, Peter," said his mother one evening, "you might as well tell us what's wrong. You've a face as long as a fiddle – it's not like you to be so down in the dumps."

"After being presented with the football trophy, you ought be walking on air. Your Mum and I were so proud of you," added his dad.

"Being presented with that cup is what the trouble is all about! I wish I'd never seen it or football!" he snapped.

"How can winning the cup be to blame?" asked his puzzled father.

Peter told them about the bullying. "I just can't understand why some of my so-called 'friends' treat me like this after we've managed to win the cup for the school," he pleaded. "They're either trying to make me lose my temper or to cry – and I'm not going to do either. I could beat any one of them in a fight!"

"I know exactly how you must feel," said his mother quickly at the mention of the word "fight", "but I really don't think that is going to solve the problem. Do you want me to write to the head teacher and ask him to look into the matter?"

"NO!" Peter snapped back angrily.

"The problem is just one word," said his father calmly, "and the word is 'jealousy'. They are making life tough for you and rejecting you because they themselves just can't take it that someone they know has done so well. Unfortunately, it's something that you have to learn about as part of growing up. It happens among grown-ups too. Kate, do you remember when I got my last promotion at work?"

"I do," said Mrs Robinson. "You were miserable for at least a week. Some of your so-called 'friends' just couldn't accept that you had got promotion instead of them."

"What happened?" asked Peter, surprised that his father should have the same problem.

"Well, I just got on with my new job and did it as well as I could," said his father. "That way they soon realised why I had been given promotion."

Peter cheered up at once to think that he was having the same problem as his Dad.

"I guess I'll just have to do the same; let them see that I'm not going to lose my temper nor cry, and just get on with things."

"That's about it, son," said his Dad.

"But do tell us if the trouble doesn't stop," added his mother.

Mr and Mrs Robinson agreed that a phone call to Peter's class teacher would be a good idea, just saying that Peter had been a bit upset lately and would he let them know if it was affecting Peter's work. All the jealousy and bullying stopped after a while. It had not been a very pleasant experience, but Peter felt that if it was all part of growing up, then it was a lesson worth learning.

*   *   *

Stimulus questions

1. Was Peter being bullied? In what ways? Why was he bullied? (jealousy)
2. Should he have told his class teacher? Why didn't he?
3. Do you know what to do if you are bullied?
4. What things helped Peter to cope? (telling parents, not being the only one, part of growing up)

Thinking time

1. Think of a time when people were very unkind to you. How did you feel? What did you do? What helped you to cope?

Prayer

"Lord, if we are bullied, make us strong and give us courage to tell people we can trust all about it. Amen."

FISHERMEN CATCH MEN
LUKE 5:1-11

THEME: **Adapting to Change**
Unexpected things may happen that mean adapting to new situations.

"It's not much fun having to wash these fishing nets when we've caught no fish," grumbled Simon Peter.

"They get just as tangled when they catch nothing but sea-weed and driftwood as they do when they're full of fish," added his brother Andrew.

"Just to think, we've been out on the Sea of Galilee all night and caught nothing," remarked James. He and his brother John were partners with Simon Peter and Andrew.

"Worse than that," added John, "everybody else has been tucked up warm in bed all night."

So they went on cleaning their nets and grumbling for all they were worth. It was a tiresome job, but the nets had to be untangled and cleaned, ready for the next fishing trip.

While they were hard at work, they noticed that they were not alone on the beach. A bit further on they saw a crowd of people listening to someone.

"I expect it's Jesus, that new teacher from Nazareth," said John.

"His father is Joseph the carpenter and his mother's Mary," added Andrew.

"We met him last week," said James. "I can't get what he said out of my mind."

"He may have said a lot of good things about the coming of God's kingdom, when justice and peace will rule," observed Simon Peter, "but right now I wish he was as good at catching fish as he is at catching a big crowd to listen to him!"

No sooner had he said this than Jesus, who was already being edged into the sea by the crowds, came over and said to Simon Peter, "I see you're not using your boats just now. Could you take me a little way out from the shore? If not, this crowd will have me up to my neck in water!"

"Gladly," said Simon Peter. "My boat might as well be used for something – it's not caught us any fish!" Simon Peter rowed out a little from the shore and Jesus continued teaching.

Not having much else to do, Simon Peter listened carefully to Jesus who was telling the crowds about the coming kingdom of God. "God wants peace and justice for all people," urged Jesus, "from the humblest fisherman up to mighty kings and emperors. It's a kingdom built on serving other people, not trying to grab as much as you can for yourself!" As he listened it began to make sense to Simon Peter. People who became powerful kings and rulers only seemed to hold their power by keeping other people poor.

When Jesus had sent the crowds home, he turned to Simon Peter and said, "What about a spot of fishing?"

Simon Peter nearly fell over the side of the boat. "What! Set out again? We've been at it all night and not even caught a sardine!" he replied rather scornfully. "But what you've been saying to the crowds seems to make sense, so I'll give it a try." He beckoned to his brother and they set off.

"Throw your nets over now," said Jesus. "It'll take both of you to pull them in."

The brothers looked at each other very doubtfully. Andrew thought to himself, "This man is the son of a carpenter – what does he know about fishing? Still, Simon Peter seems to trust him so we'd better do as he says."

"I don't know what's making it so hard to pull the nets back in," grumbled Andrew. "Perhaps they've got caught on something."

"You'll see in a minute," smiled Jesus.

Sure enough, as they kept on pulling, they saw the first of the silver fish gleaming in the sunlight.

"Wow," they shouted, "we fish all night when the fish come up to feed, and catch nothing. Then we go out in bright sunshine, when all the fish swim to the bottom, and our nets are full!" The nets were so heavy with wriggling fish that they thought they were going to break. So they called to James and John to come and help land the catch. Both boats were so full of fish that it took all their skill to stop them capsising.

This was all too much for Simon Peter, who fell down on his knees and cried, "Lord, I don't deserve this. Something has happened that I don't quite understand. What is it all about?"

"Don't be afraid," said Jesus in a firm but kind voice. "From now on you'll be catching people for God's kingdom."

The four did some rapid thinking. Jesus was so right about peace and justice for all – this is what they had been waiting for. But they were only fishermen, with not much education. If Jesus could help them catch fish, then perhaps he could use their fishing skills to help them learn how to catch people for the kingdom of God. What a change of life, but what a challenge!

The four looked at each other – there was no need to say anything – they could guess what was in each other's minds. So they pulled their boats well up the beach, gathered their cloaks and said to Jesus, "We're ready!"

* * *

Stimulus questions

1. Why did Simon Peter and Andrew have to clean their fishing nets when they hadn't caught anything? Have you ever had to do a messy job that just had to be done?

2. Why was Simon Peter so surprised when Jesus said, "What about a spot of fishing?"?

3. How would you explain what Jesus meant when he said, "From now on you'll be catching people for the kingdom of God"?
4. How would their life as fishermen help them to catch people for God's kingdom?

Thinking time

1. Think of something that you are good at. How could this be used to help other people?

Prayer

"Lord, thank you for all the gifts and skills you have given us. Help us to learn what they are and how we can use them to help others. Amen."

GRANDMA TAYLOR COMES TO LIVE WITH THE ROBINSONS

THEME: **Adapting to Change**

Being part of a family can mean making sacrifices.

Mrs Robinson had obviously been crying. When Peter, Sarah and Jemma (who was only six) came down for breakfast, they could see that their Mum's eyes were quite red and Dad was very quiet. Jemma, who was usually the first to say something, blurted out, "Mummy, why have you been crying? Have you and Daddy quarrelled?"

"Of course not, darling – whatever gave you that idea? But you'd better all sit down – we've got some bad news to tell you," said their Mum gravely.

The three children sat down, wondering whatever could have happened. Steve Robinson put his arm on Kate's shoulder as she began to explain.

"You know that Grandma Taylor, my Mum, has been living on her own since Grandad Taylor died about five years ago. Well, unfortunately Grandma has had a stroke – that means she can't walk or speak properly..."

"Is she going to die?" Jemma butted in once again.

"Of course she isn't," said Mr Robinson hastily. "She's very poorly and is in hospital, but the doctors think she will make a good recovery in time."

"But she won't be able to live on her own any longer," added Mrs Robinson. "Daddy and I have been discussing what we can do. That's what has made me so upset this morning."

"I've got a good idea," suggested Jemma. "Instead of just coming to visit us, why doesn't she come and live here always?"

"That's a very kind thought, Jemma," Mrs Robinson

replied warmly. "That's just what Dad and I have been thinking about."

"It seems the only answer," said Dad, "and I saw all your eyes light up when Jemma made the suggestion. But have you considered the implications."

"The impli... what?" queried Jemma.

"I mean," explained Dad, "that it would involve big changes for all of us."

"What sort of changes do you mean, Dad?" asked Sarah.

"Well, for a start," he went on, "where is she going to stay? Each of you has a bedroom and we haven't got a spare one. You two girls would have to share a bedroom, for a start."

The two sisters looked at each other and a frown crossed their brows.

"Sharing is all right for a while," said Sarah, "but if we have to move all Jemma's toys and things into my room, there just isn't going to be room."

Peter breathed a sigh of relief. He didn't have a brother, so he wouldn't have to share his room.

"And before you think it won't involve you, Peter," said his father, "there's going to be no more playing your CDs at full volume – Grandma will want plenty of peace and quiet."

"And there's things like TV," added Mum. "We have enough fighting already about which channel we're going to watch. You know that Grandma's favourite programme is *Emmerdale* – that's bound to clash with someone's choice."

"And what about holidays?" added Mr Robinson. "We can't just go off on some adventure holiday and leave Grandma on her own. What starts out as a good idea has got all sorts of problems. It can only work if all of us are prepared to make changes and to try to think of Grandma besides ourselves."

There was quite a long pause while everyone thought. Finally Peter broke the silence and said, "Why can't she go and live with Aunty Jane and Uncle Jim?"

"I think that's quite enough," Mr Robinson said, as he saw Mum begin to cry again.

The three children went up to their rooms.

"That was very unkind, Peter," snapped Sarah. "You made Mum cry again."

"Well, what other answer is there? Can you think of anything?" replied Peter guiltily.

"We really ought to look after Grandma," said Jemma sadly. "If it wasn't for Grandma marrying Grandad and having Mummy, and then Mummy marrying Daddy and having us, we wouldn't be here!"

"That's right, I suppose," admitted Peter. "I never looked at it that way."

"It's what being part of a family is all about, isn't it?" said Sarah, who thought carefully about most things before saying anything. "Grandma Taylor has done a lot for us."

"Yes," came back Jemma, "I like her because you can tell her all your secrets and she won't tell anyone else."

"She's the sort of person," added Peter, "that you can talk to about any problem you might have. She doesn't come back with an answer straightaway, like Mum and Dad always do. She'll listen, and ask you to explain what you mean and ask you how an idea might work out, and, before you know it, you've solved the problem yourself!"

"I think those things are much more important than which TV programme we watch," Sarah said, "and more important than having to turn the volume of your CD player down," she added, looking at Peter.

"You're right," said Peter. "Are we agreed then that we go and tell Mum and Dad that we want Grandma to stay with us?"

"Agreed," shouted Sarah and Jemma together.

"But it's not going to be easy for any of us," warned Sarah. "We're bound to get things wrong at first, but we've got to try to make it work, for Grandma's sake."

"It's all part of what being a family is all about," they all agreed.

The three bounded downstairs again into the kitchen and made their announcement.

"That's the spirit," said Dad, as he gave Peter a broad grin and Mum hugged the two girls.

* * *

Stimulus questions

1. Why did the three children like Grandma Taylor so much?
2. When they thought about it, why were they not so keen for Grandma Taylor to live with them?
3. What made them change their minds?
4. Have you ever had someone living with you for a long time? How did it affect you?

Thinking time

1. Think of a time when you had to give way to a brother or sister. How did you feel?
2. Can you always have your own way when you belong to a family?

Prayer

"Lord, we thank you for our families. Help us to learn how to care for each other, even when it means that we can't have our own way all the time. Amen."

JESUS HEALS A PARALYSED MAN LUKE 5:17-26

THEME: **Determination**

Determination to help is a sign of true friendship.

The four friends: Dan, Joel, Amos and Ben, were not looking very happy.

"They say the doctors can't do anything more to help him," sighed Dan.

"He's gradually been getting worse for years, but these last few months he's got so much worse," said Joel. "The doctors don't know what could have caused the problem."

"He can't even walk at all, not even with a stick," added Amos.

"I really don't know what's going to become of him now. He lies on his sleeping mat from morning till night, quite unable to get up," said Ben, shaking his head.

"If it wasn't for us taking it in turns to bring him his meals, I don't know how he'd survive at all," commented Dan.

The four friends were talking about Thomas, an old man who was now completely paralysed. They'd known him for many years and he had become one of their close friends.

"You feel so helpless," groaned Joel. "We've been his friends all these years and when he really needs us, there seems nothing that we can do."

"It should be at times like this that real friendship matters most, but I've no idea what we could do to help, other than making sure he has some food and a bit of company," said Amos.

"I've just thought of something," Ben said suddenly. "You know that teacher from Galilee, Jesus they call him, well, I've heard that he has cured people of all sorts of complaints."

"I've heard about him," said Dan. "Somebody in the market the other day said he had arrived in our village and all the lawyers from miles around were gathering to hear him teach."

"If he's teaching, he might not be interested in helping Thomas," said Joel doubtfully. "We couldn't very well barge in while he's having deep discussions with the lawyers."

Ben, standing up straight and looking at the other three said, "And why not? If he's helped other people why shouldn't he help poor old Thomas?"

"And how's Thomas going to get there when he can't even stand up?" complained Dan.

"Because we are going to take him to this man Jesus," replied Ben. "This calls for real determination. Who says we have a go?"

Ben was a natural leader and it didn't take him long to persuade the other three. "Right," said Ben, "we need a bit of organisation. Dan, you find out exactly which house Jesus is at. Joel, you make some sort of wooden frame that we can put Thomas's sleeping mat on. Amos, you come with me and we'll tell Thomas what we have in mind."

So plans were made. Thomas was so grateful that his friends were prepared to go to all this trouble to try to help him. "I really do hope that your determination will be rewarded," he said as the four carefully lifted his sleeping mat on to the wooden frame that Joel had made.

Soon they set off. Each of them carried a corner of the frame and Dan gave directions to the house where Jesus was. All went well until they got to the house. Jesus was inside, teaching that God's kingdom was about peace and justice and doing practical things to help the needy, not about obeying the tiny details of obscure laws. The house was full of lawyers and a large crowd had gathered outside, trying to hear what was going on.

"Oh dear," sighed Dan, "we've come all this way and can't get anywhere near."

"Nobody will let us through," said Joel, "and we can't very well barge through."

"Well, we're not giving up so easily," said Ben bravely. "Put your thinking caps on – there must be some way we can get Thomas to see Jesus."

"It might seem a wild idea," muttered Amos, "but all these houses round here have got stairs built on the outside so that people can get straight up to the flat roof. They take their crops there to store and dry them, and sometimes people sleep up there when it's very hot."

"So, your idea is to take Thomas up the outside of the house onto the roof," guessed Joel.

"That's all right, but what do we do when we get him on the roof?" questioned Dan.

"I've got an idea about that," said Ben with a twinkle in his eye. "Come on, let's waste no more time."

So they gently carried Thomas up the stairs, being careful not to tip him off his sleeping mat. Amos was right; there were all sorts of things on the roof spread out to dry in the sun.

"Now," whispered Ben, "these roofs are covered with tiles that can easily be taken off. If we remove a few we shall be able to lower Thomas down to where Jesus is!"

So very carefully and quietly they stacked some of the roof tiles in one corner and with a rope at each corner of the wooden frame they gently lowered Thomas down. The babble of noise down below suddenly stopped and 20 pairs of wide eyes and 20 open mouths looked up in amazement at what was coming down! When Thomas was finally on the ground, Jesus could see at once what was wrong with him. He not only needed help to walk again, he needed cleaning up inside. Then, looking up at the four friends who were peering down from the roof, Jesus said warmly, "Your determination has certainly helped him!" and turning to Thomas he said, "Now, get up, pick up your mat and go and start a new life!" Thomas did just that! He quickly scrambled to his feet, a bit unsteady at first, rolled up his sleeping mat and with a look of real thanks to Jesus, made his way out of the house where his four friends were waiting for him.

"That's what I mean when I say the kingdom of God is about helping people in need," Jesus said to the astonished lawyers.

Outside, Thomas and his four friends were singing and praising God for all they were worth. "We've seen remarkable things today," they said to one another. "Yes," said Ben, "you could tell that Jesus liked our determination; we just turned up at the right moment for him to show the lawyers that God's kingdom is about practical help for those in need."

* * *

Stimulus questions

1. How can you tell that the four friends really cared for the paralysed man?
2. What problems did they have in getting their friend to Jesus? How did they overcome them?
3. What did Jesus mean when he said to the four friends, "Your faith has healed him"?

Thinking time

1. Think of a time when you faced some difficulty. How did your determination overcome the problem? Did your friends help? How?

Prayer

"Lord, when our friends face difficulties, give us the determination and courage to help them in any way we can. Amen."

SARAH'S SALE

THEME: **Determination**

Determination can overcome problems.

"…And do you know what, Mum," said Sarah excitedly, "some children can't go to school because their parents are too poor to pay." Sarah, who was eight years old, had rushed in from school and not stopped talking from the minute she took off her coat.

"But Sarah, dear," interrupted Mrs Robinson, "all children in our country go to school; it's not a matter of whether their parents can pay or not."

"I don't mean in our country," Sarah went on impatiently. "I mean in lots of other countries. We had this man at assembly today, who told us all about it."

"Oh, I'm sorry, dear," said her mother. "What else did this man have to say?"

"Well, he said we could sponsor a boy or girl to help pay for them to go to school," replied Sarah. "They would write to us and we could write back to them. It costs £25 a year."

"That sounds a good idea," said her mother, "but £25 is a lot of money."

"Well, my friends Jane and Melanie and I went to see Mr Wheeler, our head teacher, to ask if we could raise the money to sponsor a girl about our age," Sarah replied quickly, "and he said it was all right, but we would have to ask our parents. So can we?"

"I suppose if Jane's and Melanie's parents agree then go ahead, but you've got to keep me in touch with what you intend to do," added her mother cautiously.

So without wasting any more time, the three girls got

started on their plans. They had a committee meeting at Sarah's house with Mrs Robinson keeping one ear on what they were deciding while she got on with writing a letter to her mother who had been ill.

"We could have a grand sale and sell things that we had made," suggested Sarah.

"I could make some Christmas cards using the pictures from last year's cards and some calendars," offered Melanie. "I'm good at art and crafts at school."

"And I could ask my Dad if he's got any plants and flowers that I could have to sell," suggested Jane. "He's got a big garden and always more plants than he knows what to do with."

"I could make some needlework things, like little purses and bookmarks," said Sarah in her turn, "and I bet my Grandma Robinson will bake some scones and cream buns."

"Where are we going to have the sale?" asked Melanie.

"I never thought about that," sighed Sarah. "I don't suppose we could have it in the house, with loads of people tramping in and out," she added, looking at her mother.

"No, dear, I don't think you could," interrupted her mother gently, "but what about asking Dad if you can use the garage?"

"That's a good idea," said Sarah with a smile, "and Peter can help Dad clear a lot of rubbish away so that we have a big space to set out all our things."

"We'll have to do some posters," suggested Melanie, "and I could get my Dad to do some letters on his computer so that we can let the houses round here know."

"What we've not decided," reminded Jane, "is when it's going to be."

"What about two weeks on Saturday?" suggested Sarah.

"That's not long to get all the preparations done," queried her mother.

"But, Mum, it's urgent – we've just got to get started," pleaded Sarah.

"Well, I can see that you are very determined, so why not?" agreed her mother.

So it was decided. Everyone had their jobs to do ready for the grand sale on Saturday 25 October, 2 pm – 4 pm. Posters were put up in the village shop and the windows of the three girls' houses. They delivered about 50 letters giving details of the grand sale to all the neighbours. Mr Robinson and Peter spent the whole of the Friday evening before the sale clearing junk out of the garage and first thing Saturday morning they took it to the tip. On the way home, they collected the scones and buns that Grandma Robinson had agreed to bake. Peter said he couldn't help with the sale because he had a football match in the afternoon. Melanie and Jane arrived about 1 pm to set things up and put price tickets on. Everything was ready by 2 pm. At 2.10 it started to rain, just drizzle at first, then it came on harder.

"Nobody's going to turn out in this," moaned Jane.

"Who wants to buy damp Christmas cards and soggy buns?" complained Melanie.

"It's no good getting fed up so soon," urged Sarah. "We've put such a lot of work into getting the sale ready – perhaps the rain will stop soon." But it didn't. At 3 pm their cash tin was empty. Mrs Robinson had been watching through the window, feeling so sorry for the girls, because they had put so much effort into raising the £25. "They'll be lucky to raise 25p," she thought to herself. "What a shame; they seem so determined." Then she had an idea. She rang a few neighbours and, after a chat, casually asked if they were planning to come to the grand sale. Some had forgotten about it, and others had been put off by the weather, but they promised they would turn out to support the girls. So they did; just a trickle of people at first and then more came. The scones were selling well, and the plants. Others quite liked the Christmas cards and needlework bookmarks. The girls were a bit happier when coins started to fall into their cash tin.

"There," said Sarah, when there was a pause. "If something is really worth doing, you've just got to stick at it. We can't let a drop of rain stop us sponsoring someone to go to school!"

At 3.45 pm people had stopped coming. "Let's count how much we've got," said Melanie, who was a lot more cheerful now. They counted and recounted.

"I make it £14.75," whispered Jane rather tearfully.

"Is that all?" said Melanie. " We're never going to get £25!"

"Well, there's still ten minutes to go," said Sarah, trying to be cheerful, but beginning to feel disappointed. "Let's not give up until the very end," she added.

Nobody else came. Just as the church clock struck four, they heard in the distance the noisy shouting of what sounded like a gang of boys. Sure enough, round the corner leading the way was Peter, plastered from head to toe in mud, followed by the rest of his team and the visiting team and their teachers.

"Are we too late for the sale?" gasped Peter out of breath. "I've told the boys that there's plenty to eat, and Granny's buns are the best in the world!" The boys bought scones, buns – and squash that Mrs Robinson had suddenly been able to produce. When the girls had sold the last of the scones and buns to the boys, the teachers had a look and bought Christmas cards, calendars, bookmarks and the rest of the plants. It was nearly 4.30 pm when they all eventually went. "Let's count the money again," said Jane excitedly. When they came to count the money, they checked and double-checked. Mr Robinson counted a third time.

"You'll never guess," said Sarah. "We've got £25.01!" she shouted happily.

"Whoopee!" screamed the other two. "Haven't we done well?"

They had done well. They were able to sponsor a girl called Naomi, who was about their age.

"I've never seen Sarah so determined about anything," Kate Robinson said to her husband Steve.

"She *must* have been determined to persuade me to clear that garage out," smiled Mr Robinson.

* * *

Stimulus questions

1. Why do you think Sarah wanted to help children she didn't even know?
2. Does your school do special things to help people in other countries?
3. How does the story show that Sarah and her friends really wanted to help other children?
4. What things happened that could have caused them to stop trying?

Thinking time

1. Think of all the good things you do at school. Think how it must feel to live in a country where children cannot go to school to learn.
2. Think what you could do to help.

Prayer

"Lord, thank you for giving us so much. Give us determination to be real friends to those in need. Amen."

JESUS INVITES MATTHEW TO BE A DISCIPLE
LUKE 5:27-32

THEME: **Friendship**

Even people who are not liked need friends.

"Where have you been all this time? Don't you know what time it is?" Japheth's wife was very angry – very, very angry. "Your dinner's in the oven, where it's been for the last three hours. I wouldn't be surprised if it's burnt to a cinder!"

Once his wife, Leah, started grumbling, it was very difficult for Japheth to get a word in edgeways. She'd got a point though. She had told him quite definitely that dinner would be ready at 6 pm and that he would have to finish work and close his tax office by 5.30 pm.

"Will you let me explain?" yelled Japheth, when Leah paused to take a breath.

"Go on then," she said, "but it had better be good."

"Well," said Japheth, "I had just dealt with my last customer, and was feeling very pleased with myself that I had so confused him that I was able to charge him twice the amount of tax that he owed. Suddenly, my friend Matthew burst in to say that he had given up being a tax collector and joined the disciples of that man called Jesus, who's been doing all those miracles and upsetting the religious leaders."

"That's a likely story," interrupted Leah. "What's that man Jesus doing asking a crooked tax collector like Matthew to join his group of friends?"

"Well, that's what I thought. Anyway, Matthew said he was having a leaving party and wanted to invite all his tax collector friends, and would I come. He said he'd explain it all on the way to his house. Well, I couldn't very well refuse, could I?"

"I suppose not," admitted Leah grudgingly.

"Well, on the way to the party at Matthew's house, he told me what had happened. Matthew had been in his tax office, cheating people and charging more tax than he should, just like we all do, when this man Jesus came in and simply said to Matthew, 'Leave all this, and follow me.' Matthew said that he'd been feeling very upset about the sort of life he had been leading – not many friends; hated by almost everyone; not trusted by anyone; never able to get anyone to help him out when he had a problem; and treated as an outcast by all the religious leaders. I know how he feels, but what else can we do? Anyway, Matthew said that he was so surprised that anyone was prepared to give him another chance in life that he just had to take it. He had heard such a lot about Jesus and the good things he had done, that if he was prepared to be friends with a crooked tax collector then there must be something in what Jesus was saying about loving God and loving your neighbour. Well, it was quite a party. All the gang of tax collectors was there, amazed to hear that Matthew was giving up the chance to make a fortune to join Jesus' band of disciples. Of course the Pharisees and the other religious leaders couldn't keep their noses out of things. 'What's your teacher doing eating with tax collectors and sinners?' they asked Jesus' disciples. They never bothered to find out what had really happened – always quick to criticise and put people down. Anyway, they got a shock. Jesus overheard them and said, 'It's not the healthy who need a doctor, but the sick. I've not come to help the proud and arrogant, but those who know they need help and don't know where to turn.'"

"Well, I never," said Leah slowly. "Wonders will never cease. But why was he talking about doctors – nobody was ill, were they?"

"Of course not," snapped Japheth, "and it had me puzzled. I've been thinking about it a lot on the way home. It is only sick people who go to the doctor. You don't go to the surgery and find it full of people who've just come to tell the doctor that they've not broken a leg, or not got a bad cough. They come because they know they need the doctor's help. I guess this Jesus is something of a doctor – not only helping to cure people with all sorts of diseases, but helping those whose lives have got into a mess. And that's how Matthew felt – that his life had gone all wrong. Nobody else was prepared to give him a second chance, except this Jesus. That's what I call being a real friend."

"I think I'm beginning to understand," said Leah quietly.

"It's made me think about our lives. If Matthew could make a fresh start, why couldn't we?" Japheth asked, looking earnestly at Leah.

"Well, come inside and while I'm clearing away the mess in the oven, we can talk about it," said Leah.

*   *   *

Stimulus questions

1. Why were tax collectors hated by almost everyone?
2. Who do you think were the only people who would be friends with them?
3. Why did the religious leaders complain when Jesus went to Matthew's leaving party?
4. Japheth and Leah started to think about their lives. Do you think they took the chance to make a fresh start?

Thinking time

1. Think how Matthew felt when Jesus gave him the chance to make a fresh start.
2. Think of a time when you hurt your friends and they were prepared to forgive you and still let you be their friend.

Prayer

"Lord, when we realise that we have hurt our friends, give us courage to go to them and put things right. Amen."

CLIVE GIVES PETER A SECOND CHANCE

THEME: **Friendship**

Even friends need to be given a second chance.

"Where's Peter?" muttered Mrs Robinson as she got the tea ready. "It's not like him to be late from school, especially when we are having his favourite – pizza with cheese and mushroom topping."

Peter was usually home from school by 4 pm. He was never later than 5 pm, even when he stayed for a football practice. It was now 5.30 pm and he was still not here.

"Did you see him leave school, Sarah?" asked her father.

"No," replied Peter's eight-year-old sister, between mouthfuls of pizza. "You know he doesn't like to walk home with me and Jemma and Mummy. Now he's nearly eleven, he thinks he's too grown up for us!"

"I knew that I shouldn't have allowed him to come home without us," sighed his mother, "but he promised he would always come home with a friend who lives in our road."

Just then they all heard the front door opening and the noise of someone going straight upstairs. "Who can that be?" said Mr Robinson. "I bet it's Peter – I'll go and investigate."

When Peter's father knocked on his bedroom door and went in, he saw Peter lying face down on his bed – he could tell that something was very wrong. It took a long time to persuade Peter to explain why he was so upset, but eventually he told his Dad what had happened.

"I was coming home from school as usual with Clive Adamson," explained Peter. "We had just crossed the road and got to the bus stop when a gang of boys from the High School got off the school bus. They stood in front of us and stopped us going any further. They took one look at Clive and told him to give them his school bag. They took his mobile phone. The biggest boy told me to clear off, if I wanted no trouble from them. I was so scared, Dad, I didn't know what to do. I know I should have stayed with Clive, but I didn't know what they might do to me – I just ran away and hid." Peter stopped and swallowed hard. "I've let my best friend down."

"But why did they pick on Clive?" asked his father.

"It's because he's black, I suppose," Peter suggested. "He was born in Birmingham, but his grandparents live in Jamaica. When they came to live here I was the first person at school to make friends with him. He's great fun to play with – and he's brilliant at football, but now I've let him down."

"I'm sure he'll understand why you had to leave him," urged his father. However, nothing could convince Peter that he had done the right thing.

Next day at school Clive tried to avoid Peter and gave him an angry look whenever they met. He didn't turn up for football practice at lunchtime either. Just before afternoon school, Peter couldn't bear it any longer. He walked up to Clive and stuttered, "I'm sorry, Clive, I didn't mean to let you down yesterday."

"Words are easy to say," snapped Clive. "It's actions that matter – and you did nothing to help." With that he walked away from Peter.

Just before the end of school, Mr Wright, their class teacher, told Peter and Clive that Mr Wheeler, the head teacher, wanted to see them both. They knew it must be to do with the incident yesterday.

"I believe you two were involved in an incident with some boys from the High School," said Mr Wheeler, looking hard at them both. They both looked down at their feet. "The head teacher at the High School thinks she knows the boys who bullied Clive and wants him to go and identify them. It's a hard thing to do, but will you do it, Clive?"

"Yes, sir," said Clive weakly.

"And I'll go with him," said Peter quickly. "It will be better if two of us identify them." Clive looked at Peter in surprise.

So it was agreed. Mr Wheeler took them next day to the High School. The two boys were introduced to Mrs Crosby, the head teacher, and they waited for the other boys to appear.

"Are these the boys who stopped you yesterday?" asked Mrs Crosby looking at Clive.

"Yes, they are," said Clive and Peter together. The boys admitted that what they had done was wrong and one of them handed back Clive's mobile phone.

"They know that they are going to be punished for breaking school rules about bullying," added Mrs Crosby, "but I want them to explain why they did it."

It was very hard for the boys to do this – much harder than just taking their punishment. They admitted that they picked on Clive because he was black. "It was because he was different from us," they explained. With Mrs Crosby's encouragement, all the boys started to talk about their feelings and the things that made them misbehave. It seemed that none of them was perfect! They all admitted to doing things they regretted later on. Peter said that he ought to have stayed with Clive and Clive said he would probably have run off if Peter had been stopped. The High School boys finally apologised to Clive and Peter and they all shook hands.

On the way back to their school, Clive looked at Peter and said, "Now I know you're a real friend – your actions proved that."

"Thanks for giving me a second chance," smiled Peter.

One day later in the summer term, Peter excitedly ran home and told his parents that Clive had asked him if he would like to go to Jamaica with them for a holiday. You can guess the rest.

* * *

Stimulus questions

1. Do you think that Peter should have stayed with Clive? Why? What else could he have done?
2. Do you know of anyone who has been bullied because of their colour?
3. Why was it especially hard for Peter to agree to go to the High School with Clive?
4. Why did they attack Clive just because he was different from them?
5. Was trying to get the boys to talk about why they did it a good way of dealing with the problem? Why?
6. What did Clive mean when he said, "Now I know you're a friend – your actions prove that"?

Thinking time

1. Think of a time when you let a friend down. How did you feel? What did you do to try to put it right?
2. If a friend let you down would you forgive them and give them a second chance?

Prayer

"Lord, when our friends let us down, give us the courage to forgive them and give them a second chance. Amen."

WISE AND FOOLISH BUILDERS
LUKE 6:46-49

THEME: **Sound Values**

Sound values may be difficult to form, but are worth the effort.

"It's all about having firm foundations," insisted David.

"That's all right," replied Dan, "but what really matters is what the building looks like above the ground!"

David and Dan were builders. They each had their own company in the same town, and they used to compete with each other in putting up the best buildings. They had quite different views about what made a good building. David always took a long time making preparations before starting, but Dan got to work almost at once and he could put up a building in no time at all. Because David took longer, he had to charge more for building a house or a barn. Because people were very impressed at the speed that Dan built, he got a lot of business. Besides, he charged a lot less than David.

They were both having a drink at the village inn after a day's work. Dan was boasting about a new house he had built.

"Well, I've finished that house – put the last window frame in this morning," said Dan proudly. "Didn't you start building one at the same time, David?"

"Yes, I did," David replied, knowing what was coming next.

"Well, I noticed that you hadn't even got the roof on yet. What's been holding you up? Have you lost your hammer?" Dan joked. David looked downcast. Dan was right – it would take him another two weeks to finish.

"But it's all about digging deep foundations," pleaded David. "That's what takes all the time."

Sam had been listening to the two arguing, as he had done

on many occasions. "Look, you two, why don't you settle your dispute once and for all?" he said.

"What do you mean?" cried out Dan and David together.

"Well, why don't you each build a house, starting at the same time, and we'll meet again a year from today to see which house is the better one," said Sam.

"Agreed," shouted Dan and David together.

So they started. In his usual way, David took a long time preparing the land for his house. He looked for a piece of land that had good solid rock beneath it. He measured the ground out carefully, and then started to dig a deep trench for the foundations. It was very hard work digging in the rocky ground. People could hear him grunting, "It's the foundations that matter" as the sweat poured from his brow.

Dan chuckled when he saw David doing all this hard work. "Fancy choosing ground which is full of rocks and boulders," he muttered to himself. "Give me nice sandy soil which is easy to dig."

So it was no surprise that Dan had finished building his house long before David had started to put the roof on his house.

"There you are," boasted Dan. "I've won the competition!"

"Not yet, you haven't," insisted David. "Sam said he wanted to see which house looked better in a year's time!"

So they waited and for a long time Dan's house looked just as good as David's. The people buying it were able to move in very quickly and only paid half what David had to charge for his house.

Soon summer was over and the winds and storms of winter began. After about a week of non-stop rain, both houses were flooded. The water rose up the walls, first ten centimetres and then before long the water was a full metre up the outside walls. One morning when it had stopped raining, and the floodwater was going down, Dan and David went out to look at their houses. Dan's house had started to tilt over at one end. He looked worried.

"It'll settle down again once the water goes down," Dan muttered to himself. David's house was as firm and steady as the day it had been built.

"It's his foundations," thought David to himself. "I've been telling him all along that it's the foundations that matter. What's the good of building a fine house if it starts tilting over as soon as any trouble arises?"

When the year had passed, Sam took Dan and David to inspect their houses. Dan's house had unfortunately not got better. It was so tilted at one end that the wall had started to collapse and the roof was caving in. David's house was as strong and sturdy as the day it was finished.

"Well, it's not hard to see who has won the competition," announced Sam. "I declare David to be the winner!"

Dan walked away feeling very sad, while David went home still muttering, "I told him it's the foundations that matter, but he wouldn't take any notice."

* * *

Stimulus questions

1. Jesus told a story like this to people who heard what he said, but didn't take any notice. Do you think he was trying to give the people a lesson in how to build houses? What might he have wanted them to build?
2. When David kept muttering, "It's the foundations that matter", what sort of things in our lives give good "foundations"?
3. When the storms came, David's house stood firm. What sort of "storms" can happen to us? What sort of values and qualities in our lives will overcome difficulties and problems?

Thinking time

1. Think of a time in your life when a difficulty or problem upset you. How did you feel?
2. What things helped you to deal with the problem?

Prayer

"Lord, help us to build our lives with strong values and qualities, so that when difficulties arise we will be able to stand firm and strong. Amen."

"IT'S THE PREPARATION THAT MATTERS!"

THEME: **Sound Values**
Careful preparation may be hard work, but it is worth the effort.

Kate Robinson was sitting in the lounge reading the school newsletter that Sarah had brought home that afternoon. They had just had tea, and Peter and Sarah, with the help of Jemma, who was only six, were clearing the table, while Mr Robinson was washing up.

"This will interest you, Sarah," said her mother. "The school would like to make a conservation area, where they can grow wild flowers and attract mini-beasts."

"That's a great idea," said Sarah excitedly. Conservation was one of Sarah's main interests, even though she was only eight.

Mrs Robinson read aloud from the newsletter: "The Parent Teacher Association are planning a sponsored cross-country race for Dads, to raise the money needed. Each sponsor agrees to pay the person they sponsor £5 if he wins, £1 if he comes in the first ten and 50p for all the rest."

Steve Robinson had finished the washing-up and, with a sigh, sank into his favourite armchair and picked up the paper.

"Dad, will you do it?" said Sarah, sitting on the arm of his chair.

"Will I do what?" he said. "I've just finished the washing-up."

"Enter the Dads' cross-country race," explained Sarah.

"Me in a cross-country race!" he exclaimed with a laugh. "I've not run a race since I left school, and that's a long time ago."

"Oh, go on," urged Peter. "I bet all the other Dads will have a go."

"Yes," added little Jemma, "I know my Daddy can run fast – he always beats me, even when he gives me a start."

What could their Dad say when all the family were persuading him to enter? He didn't want to disappoint them, especially Sarah, who wanted to do all she could to support the conservation area at school. Peter and Sarah agreed to collect sponsors for him and Jemma said she would cheer as loudly as she could.

Next morning at breakfast, Mr Robinson was missing.

"Where's Dad?" asked Peter between mouthfuls of Weetabix.

"He's out training," said Mrs Robinson with a smile.

"But, Mum, the race isn't for another three weeks," Sarah added.

"All last night your father kept saying, 'It's the preparation that matters'," she replied.

It was just the same the next morning. Mr Robinson staggered in just as they were finishing breakfast. He was quite out of breath and panting heavily.

"Is this really necessary, Steve?" complained Mrs Robinson. "You look tired out."

"It's the preparation that matters," he gasped, and then collapsed into a chair.

So it went on every day. What the children noticed, however, was that each morning their father arrived back a bit sooner. After two weeks he even got back before they had started breakfast.

"You see, it's the preparation that counts," is all he kept saying.

Derek Sawyer was another of the Dads taking part in the cross-country race. Mr Sawyer worked for the same firm as Mr Robinson and they used to have their sandwiches together at lunchtime.

"Eh, Steve," said Derek with a grin, "was that you I saw this morning, running round the park in the pouring rain? You're not training for the London Marathon, are you?"

"No, Derek," replied Steve Robinson, blushing with embarrassment, "it's this Dads' cross-country race that my kids have persuaded me to take part in – I'm trying to get fit."

"Really," exclaimed Derek with an even broader grin. "Well, if I were you I wouldn't bother. You see I'm running in it, and in my youth I was the county champion sprinter over 100 metres. If you are determined to run, I'll sponsor you since you've not much chance of winning."

Finally, the day of the race arrived. Peter and Sarah had got quite a lot of sponsors for their Dad, and, of course, Derek Sawyer's name was on their list! There were about 20 Dads taking part. Steve Robinson arrived with an old raincoat over his shorts and T-shirt, proudly accompanied by Kate his wife, and Peter, Sarah and Jemma, who had already started cheering her Dad. Derek arrived in a brand-new Adidas tracksuit with his "County Champion" badge stitched on the front. Mr Wheeler, the head teacher, blew the whistle and off they set, with Derek Sawyer taking the lead as if he was running the 100 metres. Gradually, Steve Robinson made his way through the field of runners and was soon in the leading group. Derek was so far ahead of them that he was completely out of sight. Steve pulled away from the leading group, and though he was puffing quite a lot he kept running strongly. As he ran he could see Derek in the distance leaning over a stile. When he caught up with him he saw that Derek was in great pain.

"What's the matter, Derek? Are you all right?" asked Steve between breaths.

"It's my leg," groaned Derek. "I think I've pulled a muscle. I can't go on."

"Well, as soon as I've finished, I'll get someone to pick you up," said Steve, and with that he set off at a brisk pace to try to catch the runner who had just overtaken him. With the winning line in sight, Steve was just ten metres behind the leading runner. He thought he would have to settle for second place, until he heard Jemma yelling at the top of her voice, "Come on, Dad!" He remembered how much they wanted him to win and he made an extra effort, and just reached the winning line first. The cheering was tumultuous and the three children grabbed hold of him. Steve let the head teacher know about Derek and he arranged for someone to pick him up by car.

You can imagine the excitement in the car on the way home.

"I've worked it out, Dad," screamed Peter, "and you'll get more than £100 in sponsor money, including Mr Sawyer's £5!"

"We're sure to be able to pay for the conservation area now," smiled Sarah.

"Perhaps you'll believe me now," said Mr Robinson, "that it's the preparation that counts."

"...and my cheering," added little Jemma with a cheeky smile.

* * *

Stimulus questions

1. What did Mr Robinson mean when he kept saying, "It's the preparation that counts"?
2. Why didn't Derek Sawyer bother to train? What might have happened if he had trained?
3. Can you think of other things that you can only do well if you work hard?

4. What sort of qualities will help you do well in life? How can you learn them?

Thinking time

1. Think of something that you have worked hard at to succeed. Was it worth the trouble?

Prayer

"Lord, give us the patience and determination to learn the values and qualities of life that will help us to overcome the problems we may face as we grow up. Amen."

JESUS HEALS THE
CENTURION'S SERVANT
LUKE 7:1-10

THEME: **Accepting Others**

Trust in someone reliable overcomes problems.

There was a gentle knock on the door and a quiet voice from inside said, "Enter!" Felix went in without a murmur and stood in front of his master, the centurion Marcus.

"Well, Felix, what's the latest news about my servant Justus?" the centurion said in a grave voice.

"I'm afraid it's bad news, sir," murmured Felix. "Justus seems to be getting worse. He had a very bad night and the doctors don't think he will live much longer."

"If Justus dies," said Marcus, "it will be a tragedy. He's one of my most faithful servants. I don't know what I shall do without him. Is there anything else we can do, Felix?"

"Well, sir," Felix replied with a note of hesitation in his voice, "there is someone who might help, but I just can't see how he could come to your house to see Justus."

"What do you mean, Felix?" the centurion said hastily. "Anyone who could help Justus to get better would be more than welcome in my house – and I would pay him well."

"But you see," explained Felix, "the person I have in mind is a Jew and you know that their laws make it very hard for them to go into the houses of non-Jews, even important Roman soldiers like you."

"I see what you mean," agreed Marcus, "but who is this man anyway?"

"His name is Jesus," replied Felix. "He's helped a lot of people who have had diseases of all kinds – but with respect, sir, I really don't think he would have anything to do with a Roman soldier."

"But wait a minute, Felix," said Marcus, "you know how well I get on with the local Jews in town. Do you think they would go for me to this Jesus and try to persuade him to come?"

"It's worth a try, sir," said Felix eagerly. "When all is said and done, you did pay for a new synagogue to be built for them."

So it was arranged. A group of Jewish leaders from the synagogue went to meet Jesus, who had just arrived in Capernaum, to try and persuade him to come to the centurion's house and help Justus, who was on the point of dying.

"We know that it's against the strict teaching of the law for a Jew to go into the house of a Roman," they explained, "but this man Marcus is a Roman centurion and has been very kind to us in many ways. He has even paid for a new synagogue to be built." The group of Jews pleaded with Jesus to help. "Though he isn't a Jew, he really deserves your help," they added. Jesus smiled at them.

"Anyone who is as kind as that shows real love, and that's the sort of person God wants to help, even though he isn't a Jew," explained Jesus. "Of course I will come at once. Show me where he lives."

Marcus was at home, anxiously waiting to see if Jesus would come. "I do want his help, but I don't want to appear rude to him by asking him to come here, when I know the Jewish law forbids it," thought Marcus to himself. So he had another plan. Meanwhile, Jesus and the others set off, but when they got near Marcus's house, another group of servants belonging to Marcus met them.

"Marcus, our master, has sent us to thank you for being willing to come to his house, but he doesn't want to be rude when he knows it is against your law to come to his house, so he sent us with this message." They carefully explained what Marcus had told them to say.

"Our master Marcus is a Roman centurion and has great power over his soldiers. If he says to any of them, 'Do this', he does it straightaway, or if he says, 'Come here', then the soldier stops whatever he is doing and comes. Well, Marcus believes that you also have great authority. He believes that if you say that his servant Justus will get well, then it will happen. This way you don't even have to come into his house."

Jesus stood still with amazement. "I've never found anyone with this kind of trust in me before," he said. "He is quite right, I have no need to come into his house, but I would very much like to meet him one day."

So they all thanked Jesus and rushed back to Marcus's house. When they saw Marcus waiting for them with a broad smile on his face and Justus standing by his side, they knew what had happened.

"I really must see this Jesus one day to thank him for all he has done," Marcus said warmly.

Some time later, when Jesus was crucified, there was a centurion on duty at the cross. Looking up at Jesus, the centurion said, "I believe this man was the Son of God." Who knows – this centurion might just have been Marcus.

* * *

Stimulus questions

1. How did Marcus, the centurion, show that he was a kind man, even to people very different from himself?
2. Why did Felix, his servant, really not believe that Jesus would come and help to heal Justus?
3. How did Marcus show that he believed Jesus could help Justus, without even having to come to his house?

4. It's not safe to trust everyone. How can you tell which people you can safely trust, if you are in difficulties or have problems?

Thinking time

1. Think of a time when something has been troubling you. How have you decided which people to trust? Think who they were and what they did to help.
2. Think of the people you can trust again if you have a problem or difficulty.

Prayer

"Lord, when we find life is hard and don't know where to turn for help, show us the people we can trust to help us. Amen."

SARAH LEARNS TO TRUST

THEME: **Accepting Others**

Learning to trust people different from ourselves is not always easy.

The Robinson children, Peter, Sarah and little Jemma, were looking forward to the half-term holiday. They were going to stay in a caravan by the sea near Torquay in Devon. They had often been there and Peter who was ten (nearly eleven as he kept reminding people) and Sarah who was eight, sometimes wished that they could go somewhere else for a change. However, little Jemma, who was six, thought it was wonderful – "It's the best seaside in the whole world," she said, quite forgetting that it was the only seaside she had ever been to!

This time things were a bit different. Peter's Mum and Dad had agreed to let him bring his friend Clive, and Sarah was excited because she had learned to swim and didn't need her arm bands in the pool any longer. She was looking forward to swimming in the sea. "It'll be very different from swimming in the leisure centre pool," warned her Mum. "You'll have to take extra care and always have someone with you who can swim well."

After a long, tiring car journey, they finally arrived at the caravan site and the children quickly unpacked their things, while Mrs Robinson prepared their favourite tea – fish fingers, beans and chips. They were always interested in finding out who was in the caravan next to theirs, so Sarah and Jemma went to explore. They were soon back with lots of things to tell the others.

"They've got two children," announced Jemma, "but they've got very strange names."

"Yes," added Sarah, "I heard the mother call one Sita and the other Raj. I think they were their names, but I've never heard anyone called that before."

"They must be an Indian family," said Clive. "We had lots of people from India and Pakistan in my last school near Birmingham. I think there were three girls called Sita and at least four boys called Raj. One of my best friends was called Raj. I missed him a lot when I had to move schools."

"Why do they have such unusual names?" Jemma asked. "We've no one called that at our school."

"Their names are only unusual because you've never heard them before," insisted Clive. "I expect 'Jemma' would sound very odd if you'd never heard it before!" Jemma looked hurt and went off to read a book.

The next morning they all went down to the beach. The family from the next caravan was already there and Sita, who was about fourteen, and Raj her younger brother were exploring the rock pools. Peter and Clive had gone further up the beach to fly Peter's kite, leaving Sarah and Jemma with their Mum and Dad. The girls were very interested in what Sita and Raj had found in the rock pools, but were not sure about going over and making friends. They watched from a distance.

"Sarah, Jemma," shouted Mrs Robinson, "it's time for the picnic. Peter and Clive are back." The girls rushed up with more news of the new family.

"The people from the next caravan are having a picnic too," announced Jemma, who never missed a thing. "I heard their mum ask the girl if she wanted 'some sauces'."

"Some what?" asked Peter.

"I expect she said 'samosas'," explained Clive, "They're very tasty. Our next-door neighbours in Birmingham were Indian and Mrs Kappur taught my Mum how to make them."

"Well, they're not a bit like proper sandwiches," pouted Jemma.

"The family do seem quite nice, really," said Sarah, "but they are so different – I don't know if I could really trust them."

"What a strange thing to say," Mrs Robinson exclaimed.

After lunch Mr and Mrs Robinson packed up the picnic things and took them to the caravan. Peter and Clive went off again to fly the kite. Jemma started to build a sandcastle, but didn't get very far because she kept glancing to see what the Indian family were doing! Sarah looked at the sea and wondered if she could try to swim. She remembered what her mother had said, but the sea seemed quite calm. She waded in and then went a bit further and a bit further, till the water came up to her shoulders. She was about to try the breaststroke when a large wave seemed to come from nowhere and swept her off her feet. Before she could do anything the wave pulled her from the shore and she found herself drifting into deep water. She swallowed a lot of water and began to panic. Each time she opened her mouth to scream it was filled with water. It was little Jemma who saw what had happened and wondered where she could get help.

"I could rush all the way up to the caravan and get Mum and Dad," she thought. But then she saw Sita. Plucking up all her courage she rushed to her and shouted, "Please help my sister, she's going to drown!" Sita quickly saw what had happened and grabbed a rubber ring that had a piece of rope tied to it. She rushed to the edge of the water, took careful aim and threw the ring out to Sarah, keeping a tight grip on the rope. Her aim was just right and Sarah was able to grab the ring. Sita pulled her carefully ashore and started to carry out the lifesaving drill she had learned. Sarah coughed up a lot of water but by the time Mr and Mrs Robinson had arrived she was feeling a lot better. They thanked Sita very much for her quick thinking and they all went to tell Sita's parents what had happened. Sarah was very sorry that she had not obeyed her parents.

"I've learned my lesson," Sarah said, "but wasn't I lucky that Sita was there to help?"

"You just had to trust her when you needed her help," said Clive, "even though she has a funny name and eats strange food," he added with a smile.

"Trusting people is not about what they eat and the names they have," said Sarah. "It's whether they help you when you need them – and Sita certainly did that!"

"Mum," whispered Jemma, "can we invite Sita and Raj to tea tomorrow – and will you make 'some sauces'?" she added with a grin.

"Samosas!" shouted Peter and Clive together.

* * *

Stimulus questions

1. What was it that made Sarah and Jemma unsure about making friends with Sita and Raj?
2. Why did Clive seem to have a different attitude towards Sita and Raj?
3. What lessons did Sarah learn about swimming? What did she learn about trusting people?

Thinking time

1. Think of a time when you got into some difficulty. How did you feel? Who helped you? How did you know you could trust them?

Prayer

"Lord, when we are in difficulty, help us to know whom we can trust to help us. Amen."

SIMON THE PHARISEE
LUKE 7:36-50

THEME: **Judging others**
It is easy to judge others and to misunderstand them.

Simon the Pharisee was having dinner with some other religious leaders, when the conversation turned to this new preacher called Jesus.

"I've heard that this Jesus mixes with all the rubbish of society – tax collectors, cheats, outcasts, and all manner of villains – the sort of people we never see worshipping God in the synagogue," commented Simon.

"But I've heard that he also heals the sick," argued Zebedee, "so surely he can't be all bad."

"But he's not a trained teacher and surely mixing with this sort of people proves he's no great prophet," insisted Simon.

"If you're so sure that he's no good," interrupted Zephaniah, "then why don't you invite him to dinner and we can decide for ourselves?"

"That's a good idea," smiled Simon. "We shall be able to trap him into admitting all sorts of things, and prove that he is a cheat. We might even get enough evidence to have him thrown into jail."

So it was arranged. Simon invited Jesus to dinner. It wasn't that he really wanted to welcome Jesus as his guest, but to give him and his friends a chance to trap Jesus. Nevertheless, Jesus accepted the invitation.

It was so warm on the evening of the dinner that they ate outside on the verandah. Everything was going quite well and Simon and his friends had started to ask a few questions. Without any warning a very anxious and frightened woman came to where Jesus was sitting. She was crying bitterly and as her tears fell on Jesus' feet she wiped them with her long hair. She opened a box of perfume and began to pour it on his feet.

Simon and his friends looked on in amazement. For once they were speechless and wide-eyed. Finally, Simon blurted out, "If this Jesus were a real prophet, he would know who this woman is – an absolute waster, who's made a complete mess of her life and the lives of others. We know her well and won't have anything to do with her!" The others nodded in agreement.

"Simon," said Jesus quite firmly, "you just listen to what I've got to say!" He stood up, with the woman by his side, and spoke to them all.

"Simon, this woman has shown me more love and respect than you ever could! You invited me to be your guest, but when I arrived, did you offer me water to wash the dust off my feet like you did your other guests? No, you didn't! But the first thing she did was to wash my feet with her tears. Did you give me a kiss of greeting when I arrived like you did your other guests? No, you didn't! But from the time this woman arrived, she was so pleased to see me that she has been kissing my feet. Did you give me some perfumed oil to refresh me after my journey like you did your other guests? No, you didn't! But she has poured perfume on my feet; it must have cost her a lot of money. You invited me here to trick me, but she came because she wanted me to forgive her past faults and help her to start a new life. You and your friends judge people by outward things, but God looks deep inside a person. I'll tell you this – you may be a Pharisee and be very religious and have lots of authority, but that counts for nothing if you have a wicked, scheming mind! You like people to bow down to you and to give you the best places at special festivals, but this counts for nothing if your heart is not right with God! God knows who is genuine and who is not."

Simon and the others were stunned. Their faces were red with shame, especially as a large crowd had now gathered.

In a much gentler voice Jesus said, "Simon, how can you

love God a lot when you don't see your need of his forgiveness? This woman has shown her great love and so her many sins have been forgiven." Turning to the woman Jesus said, "You have shown that you are truly sorry for all the things you have done wrong. Your sins are forgiven. Go, and with God's help, start a new life."

Simon and his friends went home with a great deal to think about.

* * *

Stimulus questions

1. How can you tell that Simon hadn't really invited Jesus as his friend? What things hadn't he bothered to do?
2. When you are invited to someone's house for a meal, what sort of things do they do to show that you are welcome?
3. Why did it take great courage for the woman to do what she did?
4. How can we easily get the wrong idea about someone, by how they look or what they wear? Can you give examples?

Thinking time

1. Think of some of the people that you don't like, just because of what other people have told you about them, or because of what they look like. Don't forget that they have feelings and can be very hurt.

Prayer

"Lord, when we are tempted to judge people by outward things, help us to remember that you look deep into a person's heart. Help us to be willing to give people a new start in life. Amen."

MOTORWAY CHASE

THEME: **Judging Others**

It is easy to get the wrong impression from what people do.

At last the summer term had come to an end and the Robinson children, Peter, Sarah and Jemma, were looking forward to the long summer holidays. "No more school for six whole weeks," shouted Peter, as he walked through the school gate and headed up the road for home. He wasn't telling anyone in particular – he just felt like shouting it out!

When he got home, after calling at the corner shop for his favourite football magazine, he found that his mother, who had already collected Sarah and Jemma from school, was busy getting the tea ready. "Come on, Peter," she said crossly, "get a move on. We've a lot to do before your father gets home. He'll expect all the packing to be done and everything ready for loading into the car. You know how bad-tempered he gets if we can't set off before all the holiday traffic jams the roads."

Peter was looking forward to their two-week caravan holiday by the sea. He was busy collecting together the things he wanted to take – football, snorkel, flippers and swimming things – when the telephone rang. When Mrs Robinson finally put the phone down she was looking very worried.

"What's the matter, Mum?" Sarah asked, between deciding what she should pack.

"It's Grandma," sighed Mrs Robinson. "Grandad has just rung to say that Grandma has had a fall and she might have to go into hospital for an operation."

"Does that mean we can't go on holiday?" piped up Jemma.

"I don't know what we should do," replied her mother.

"Grandad says we mustn't let this spoil our holiday. He says we can always phone to see how she is getting on, but I don't know."

When Steve Robinson rushed in from work, Kate told him the bad news. "I'm sure Grandma wouldn't want to spoil our holiday," he said, "but we must phone every day just to see that she is all right."

"Don't forget to take your mobile phone with you," Peter reminded him.

Soon everything was packed – including the mobile phone – and they set off. The traffic was not too bad and they soon got to the motorway services where they stopped for a drink. They had to share a table with a man who was wearing a black leather jacket and trousers and whose long greasy hair was tied back with a piece of dirty string. He kept eyeing Mr Robinson's mobile phone. "Better give Grandad a ring," said Mr Robinson, "to see how Grandma is."

"She's quite comfortable in bed," he told them. "Now let's press on so we get to the caravan before dark."

They had not gone far up the motorway when they heard a roar behind them.

"It's only a motorbike," said Peter. "Looks like he's trying to overtake us, Dad."

"No motorbike is going to pass me!" Mr Robinson responded, putting his foot down.

"Now he's flashing his headlights," announced Sarah.

"Isn't it that nasty man who was at our table in the service station?" observed Jemma.

"I believe you're right," said her mother turning round. "I wonder what he's trying to do? I thought he looked a bit suspicious. He never took his eyes off the mobile phone."

"Perhaps he's trying to hold us up and steal the phone and all our money, just like an old-fashioned highwayman!" blurted out Peter excitedly.

Just then the man on the motorbike started to overtake

them and kept pointing at Mr Robinson and trying to say something. He swerved his bike close to the side of the car.

"If he thinks he's going to force me onto the hard shoulder, he's wrong!" shouted Mr Robinson. "I'll show him." With that he drove the car even faster.

"Do be careful, Steve," pleaded Mrs Robinson. "We mustn't have an accident." The children in the back were wide-eyed with excitement. Nothing like this had ever happened before.

However hard he tried to pull away from the motorbike, Mr Robinson's car was no match for this 1,000 cc Kawasaki. The motorbike pulled in front of them and tried to make them slow down.

"I know what I'll do," said Mr Robinson nervously, "I'll pull off at the next junction and try to give him the slip." The motorbike pulled alongside again and the man waved his arms furiously. At the turn off, Mr Robinson yanked his steering wheel sharply to the left, but the motorbike was so quick he followed him up the slip road.

"I'll have to try to shake him off somehow," said Mr Robinson defiantly. He made a left turn and then a right turn and left again and braked hard before turning off the engine. They waited patiently, their hearts pounding with excitement and fear.

"I'm frightened," whimpered Jemma.

"I can see him coming," shouted Peter.

"Right, that's enough," Mr Robinson said angrily. "I'm phoning the police. Where's my mobile?" He couldn't find it in his pocket, nor in the glove box. As they were all hurriedly searching for the mobile, there was a screech of brakes followed by a sharp tap on the car window. It was the man from the motorway services. Mr Robinson wound down his window about five centimetres. "Now look here, just what do you think you're up to?" he bellowed.

"What's all the hassle, mate?" said the biker with a puzzled expression on his face.

"If I could find my mobile," replied Mr Robinson, "the police would be after you!"

"You won't find your mobile," grinned the biker, "'cos you left it on the table at the motorway services. I've had a terrible job trying to catch you up to give it back to you." With that he slipped the mobile through the gap in the window.

"Er, thanks very much," Mr Robinson muttered feebly, "it's good of you to bother." The Robinsons had a lot to talk about *and* to think about on their way to the caravan.

* * *

Stimulus questions

1. What things made the Robinsons suspicious of the biker when they were in the motorway services? What else could Mr Robinson have done when he was followed on the motorway?
2. What sort of things might each of the Robinsons have said to each other after the incident?
3. What other kinds of people are misunderstood because of what they wear or do or say?

Thinking time

1. Think of some of the people who are misunderstood. Imagine what they feel like.

Prayer

"Lord, forgive us when we judge people wrongly. Help us to look at a person's attitude and behaviour, not what they wear or the colour of their skin. Amen."

JESUS CALMS THE STORM
LUKE 8:22-25

THEME: **Facing Difficulties**
Difficulties can be overcome by trusting people who are reliable.

"I've never seen so many people in all my life," declared Peter, looking at the vast crowds that had gathered to listen to Jesus.

"Well, Jesus did say that we would be catching people instead of fish, so we mustn't be surprised at the crowds," joined in James, another disciple who used to be a fisherman.

"But this is getting quite out of hand," argued Thomas. "How can he deal with so many people at once? They're all pushing to get to him. I'm surprised he can hear what they say."

Jesus sensed that the disciples were worried. So he said to them, "What about having a few days' holiday away from the crowds?"

"That sounds a great idea," they all chorused.

"But how are we going to give all these people the slip?" complained Thomas. "They'll follow us wherever we go."

"What about a trip to the other side of the lake?" suggested Jesus. "I don't think they'll follow us there, because it's not a Jewish area, and you know what our people are like for keeping themselves to themselves."

"That's a great idea," Peter said enthusiastically. "I know where I can borrow a boat from for a few days." So off he went to make arrangements.

The lake that Jesus mentioned was very large; in fact it was called the Sea of Galilee, and there was one thing about the Sea of Galilee that made it very dangerous. The lake was surrounded by hills, and when the wind got up it would blow like a whirlwind and create a sudden storm. There wasn't very much warning, and the storm could suddenly calm down as quickly as it had arisen.

Peter got the boat and, being a fisherman, he took charge, of course. It was quite a pleasant afternoon when they started and they were all glad to escape the crowds.

"How peaceful it is out here," commented Thomas. "Just to think that a few minutes ago we were surrounded by the noisy crowds."

"It's peaceful all right," smiled James. "Have you noticed Jesus? He's in the back of the boat with his head on a cushion, fast asleep!"

"He must be worn out," said Philip. "I don't know how he manages to keep going, day after day. Don't disturb him. Peter knows all about boats and this lake, so we are in safe hands."

A few minutes later things changed. First, the sun went behind a cloud, and then there were little gusts of wind – nothing very much, but enough to make the waves slap the side of the boat. Peter worked hard to keep the boat steady, but things got worse. The little gusts of wind became a gale and the waves that were slapping the side of the boat were now washing into the boat. The boat rocked from side to side and whatever Peter did made no difference at all.

"Don't worry, lads," shouted Peter, "I've had to deal with worse weather than this."

"I don't know how Jesus can still be asleep with all this racket going on," said Matthew.

They all started to bale out the water from the boat, but the sea was washing into the boat quicker than they were able to empty it out. All this time Jesus was fast asleep.

"I can't do anything more," shouted Peter above the noise of wind and waves. "This is far worse than anything I've had to deal with."

"We shall just have to wake Jesus," said Thomas.

The disciples shook Jesus vigorously to wake him up.

"Master, master," they shouted, "we're going to drown. Don't you care? How can you still sleep when we're all in danger?"

Jesus roused himself, steadied himself by grabbing the side of the boat and then shouted out, "Now that's quite enough of that! Calm down again and let us continue our journey in safety!"

In a minute or two, the howling wind became little gusts and the waves that were coming over the sides of the boat were gently slapping the side. In another minute the clouds parted and the sun shone and the lake was like a pond.

"That's better," said Jesus cheerily. "Now let's be on our way."

The disciples looked at each other speechlessly, but it was Peter as usual who was the first to speak.

"I...I...don't know what's happened, lads, but it looks as if we shall make it to the other side after all."

"Of course we shall," said Jesus. "Where is your faith? Did you really think that I had called you all to be my disciples just to let you all drown? When are you going to learn to trust me? There will be worse things than this for you to cope with, so start learning to trust me straightaway!"

The disciples looked at each other in amazement.

"Who is this," they said to one another, "that even the wind and the sea obey him?"

"I can see we've a lot to learn about being disciples," admitted Peter, "but what's happened today has given us all a lot to think about. This Jesus is no ordinary person. I wonder what he meant when he said that there would be worse things than this for us to cope with?"

* * *

Stimulus questions

1. Huge crowds of people followed Jesus. What is the biggest crowd you have ever been in? What was it like? Were you frightened? Was there someone with you to help?
2. Peter was expert at sailing on the Sea of Galilee. Have you ever been sailing? What things have you to check first?
3. Jesus wasn't a sailor like Peter, but he was someone very special who could help in all kinds of difficulties. Why would it be hard for Peter to trust Jesus?
4. If you have a problem or something that is troubling you, do you have people that you know you can trust to help?

Thinking time

1. Think of a time when you have been lost in a crowd. How did you feel? What did you do? Who helped you?
2. Think of a time when you were frightened about something. How did you feel? Think of the people you can trust to help you, and say a quiet "thank you" to them in your heart.

Prayer

"Lord, when we are afraid and don't know what to do, show us someone we can trust to help us. Thank you for those people who have helped us when we were anxious or in difficulty. Amen."

RAVI PATEL'S PACKED LUNCH

THEME: Facing Difficulties

Difficulties can be overcome by trusting real friends.

"Don't be late for the school trip tomorrow, Peter," shouted Ravi Patel as he and Peter Robinson went their separate ways home after school.

"And don't you forget to bring a packed lunch this time," Peter shouted back with a grin. "You forgot it last time and had to share mine!"

The Patel family had only recently moved house, and when Ravi joined Peter's class at King's Road Primary School, they soon became good friends. It was the last week of the summer term and they were both looking forward to their class visit to a nearby water park. The Robinsons and the Patels had got to know each other quite well. Ravi was in Peter's class and Nisha, Ravi's younger sister, was in Sarah's class. Besides this, Mr Robinson often went to town on Saturday morning and bought tools and electrical things from Mr Patel's shop.

"Mum, will you get me a packed lunch ready for tomorrow's trip, please?" Ravi asked, as soon as he got home. "I'd better not forget it again – Peter Robinson won't want to share his lunch with me a second time!"

"You're lucky to have a friend like Peter," replied Mrs Patel. "It's not everybody who would share their lunch. I shall need to leave for work just before you go to school, but I'll leave your lunch in a carrier bag on the kitchen table. Put it in your school bag with all your other things – and *don't forget it!*"

Next morning, Ravi was up extra early, eagerly looking forward to the school trip. His mother, who was a nurse at the hospital, had already gone to work, and Mr Patel had set off to the shop. Ravi and Nisha had their breakfast and got their things ready for school. They usually walked to school with the family next door.

"And have you got your packed lunch?" Nisha reminded Ravi.

"Oh, thanks for remembering," said Ravi, and he dashed into the kitchen and grabbed a carrier bag. It was quite heavy, but he knew his mother always gave him plenty of his favourite samosas and pitta bread filled with spicy chicken.

Ravi and Peter sat together on the coach and the journey to the water park quickly passed.

"Don't forget to take all your things with you," said Mr Wright, their class teacher, "especially your packed lunches!"

"Are you sure you've remembered your lunch this time?" said Peter, looking at Ravi.

"Of course I have," replied Ravi impatiently. "This bag weighs a ton!"

They had a great morning at the water park. There were canoes, rowing boats and lots of water birds to identify. There was an area for swimming and an endurance course. The morning passed very quickly, but they were ready for lunch when Mr Wright blew his whistle. Ravi and Peter found a grassy spot in the shade and started to search for their lunch bags. Peter opened his and started on his sandwiches and crisps without waiting for Ravi. Ravi pulled out the heavy carrier bag, opened it and froze to the spot. His hands started to quiver and his whole body trembled.

"What's the matter, Ravi?" said Peter between mouthfuls. "You've not forgotten your lunch again, I hope!"

"I...I...I...don't know what's happened," Ravi stuttered, "but something's gone wrong and I'm going to be in serious trouble." He could hardly hold back his tears.

"It can't be so bad," joked Peter. "You're not going to burst into tears just because your Mum hasn't packed your favourite samosas!"

"Look!" murmured Ravi. "What am I going to do, Peter?" Ravi was still shaking as he opened the carrier bag for Peter to look inside.

"Wow!" exclaimed Peter. "Where did you get all that money from?"

"I didn't take any money," Ravi exclaimed. "I just picked up my packed lunch."

"There must be hundreds of pounds," said Peter quietly.

"What am I going to do?" Ravi said. "I can't go home – my family will think that I have stolen the money. I have brought shame and disgrace on all my family," he whimpered.

"Don't be silly, Ravi," Peter said, trying to reassure him. "They will understand that some mistake has happened. They know you wouldn't steal all this money."

"But I just can't go back and face them. They'll think I stole the money and then got scared and then made up some excuse about getting the wrong bag," Ravi insisted.

"You need someone you can trust to speak to your parents and explain how upset you are and that some mistake has happened," said Peter firmly, "and I know who that someone is!"

"Who do you mean?" Ravi said, looking up hopefully.

"Mr Wright, our class teacher, of course," replied Peter. Peter and Ravi went to where Mr Wright was just finishing his sandwiches and explained what had happened.

"Don't worry, Ravi," said Mr Wright, "I'll ring your home on my mobile and say how upset you are. I've no idea what's happened, but I'm sure your Mum and Dad will be able to explain. At least they will know that you have owned up to the mistake." They waited patiently while Mr Wright rang Ravi's home. He soon returned with a broad smile on his face.

"You thought your father would be angry, didn't you, Ravi?" beamed Mr Wright. "Well, he's a very happy man! He was just about to report to the police that £650 had been stolen.

Your mother was quite upset too – you left your packed lunch on the kitchen table!" Mr Wright explained that when Ravi's father had come home from the shop very late, he had left all the day's money from the shop in a carrier bag on the kitchen table. Ravi had taken the wrong bag! Ravi gave a deep sigh of relief and showed the faintest signs of a smile.

"You'll have to learn to find people you can trust," said Peter. "If Mr Wright hadn't been here you might have run off to Timbuktu! And now I suppose I'll have to share my lunch with you – *again!*" he added with a grin.

* * *

Stimulus questions

1. Ravi seemed to be quite a forgetful person. Are you like him? What have you forgotten?
2. Why was Ravi so scared? Do you think his family would think he had stolen the money?
3. How was Mr Wright able to help Ravi, when he didn't know what had happened?

Thinking time

1. Think of a time when you were scared to own up to something. How did you feel? What did you do? Was there someone you could trust to help? What happened?
2. Think of the people that you could trust to help you if something like this happened again.

Prayer

"Lord, when we are afraid and don't know where to turn for help, show us someone we can trust, to whom we can talk. Thank you for people who helped us when we were in difficulty. Amen."

JAIRUS'S DAUGHTER
LUKE 8:40-56

THEME: **Care and Compassion**

Care and compassion can help people cope with difficulties.

"It just doesn't seem fair," wept Naomi. "For years we didn't have any children at all and then God answered our prayers and gave us a little girl – the only child I was able to have."

"I know how you feel, dear," said Jairus, trying to comfort his wife.

"And then this tragedy happens", and Naomi burst into tears again.

"It does seems strange," reflected Jairus. "We were so thrilled when she was born and we have loved her and cared for her for the past twelve years – and then this!"

"And you being the leader of the synagogue seems to make no difference. You would think that God would care for his special servants," argued Naomi.

"I know what you mean, Naomi," said Jairus, "but perhaps God thinks that his special servants are able to cope with tragedies like this. I'm not sure that we should expect special treatment." Whatever Jairus said and did to comfort Naomi seemed to make no difference.

The tragedy that had happened to their daughter was that she had suddenly become very ill. They had a number of doctors to visit her, but none was able to say what was wrong. They tried all sorts of medicines, but nothing seemed to work. The little girl gradually got weaker and weaker. Jairus and Naomi were getting desperate.

Then one day Jairus heard that Jesus was back in town. He had heard quite a lot about him, but didn't really know what to make of the stories that he had healed the lame and helped the blind to see again. Crowds of people were flocking to see him. One evening while they were at their daughter's bedside, Jairus and Naomi were talking about Jesus and the stories about him.

"We could do with this Jesus curing our daughter," said Jairus with a deep sigh, "but I don't expect he'd be interested in me. Anyway, I don't want to look a fool if all these stories about what he has done aren't true."

"Yes, dear," agreed Naomi, "we've had enough worry already. I don't think I could take another disappointment." Together they looked at their daughter, lying so still and looking so pale. They looked at each other and seemed to know what the other was thinking when they both said together, "But it's worth a try!"

"Looking at our only child lying there, so still, makes me so sad that I don't mind being a fool if this Jesus can help," added Jairus. With that he grabbed his cloak and set off to find Jesus.

He followed the crowds and sure enough, there was Jesus in the middle, talking to them and answering their questions. Jairus just heard the end of a conversation Jesus was having with a group of women. "God does care for us, especially when we are faced with great problems," Jesus said.

"That's what I need," thought Jairus, and pushing his way to the front of the crowd, he fell down at Jesus's feet and said, "Please come and help my little daughter. I think she's going to die! She is the only child God has given us and now he is taking her from us. Please come!"

Jesus needed no further persuasion and set off at once with his disciples and Jairus. They made slow progress because of the crowds. As they turned into the road where Jairus lived, they were met by one of Jairus's neighbours who had been with Naomi.

"It's too late," she shouted. "Your daughter has just died. There's no point in Jesus bothering to come now!"

When Jesus heard this and saw the look of horror on Jairus's face, he turned to him, and looking into his eyes said, "Jairus, don't be afraid; just believe and she will be healed."

They arrived at the house and Jesus took Peter, James and John, three of his disciples, and Jairus inside. The people outside had already started wailing and crying, but inside it was quiet and calm.

He went with Jairus and Naomi to the girl's bedside and looking at the parents with great love in his eyes, he took hold of the little girl's hand and said quietly, "Come on, dear, it's time to wake up." The little girl rubbed her eyes, opened them wide and sat up. Jairus and Naomi were speechless with wonder.

"Hadn't you better get her something to eat?" Jesus said with a smile. "She's bound to be hungry after being ill so long."

At once Naomi set about getting her favourite meal ready, while Jairus thanked Jesus, though he hardly knew what words to say.

"It's been a very difficult time for you and Naomi," said Jesus. " It will take you a long time to understand what has happened. Keep this to yourselves and remember that God gives us strength to cope with problems whether they end in happiness or sadness."

* * *

Stimulus questions

1. Why did Naomi think that God was being unfair to them?
2. What was it that made Jairus seek Jesus' help?
3. Why do you think Jesus took Peter, James and John into the house?

4. What do you think Jesus meant when he said to Jairus, "God gives us strength to cope with problems whether they end in happiness or sadness"?

Thinking time

1. Think of someone you know who is very ill. Think of the things that family and friends do to help.
2. What could you do?

Prayer

"Lord, when we see people in need, help us to care for them, and show us what we can do to help. Amen."

SALLY'S SPECIAL GIFTS

The Robinson family were having tea. It wasn't very often that they all had their tea together; sometimes Mr Robinson was working late, sometimes Mrs Robinson was on duty at the hospital, and sometimes the three children had their tea as soon as they came home from school and their Mum and Dad had theirs later. Just for once, they all sat down together for the children's favourite meal – chicken nuggets, chips and beans, followed by chocolate fudge cake. Peter and his little sister Jemma were arguing about who was going to have first turn on the computer, but their sister Sarah was eating her tea without saying a word, which was very unusual for her.

"You're quiet tonight, Sarah," enquired her mother. "Is something wrong?"

"No, Mum," Sarah replied, "it's just that it doesn't seem right really."

"What's not right?" asked her Dad.

"Well, someone new has started school and she's in my class," explained Sarah.

"What's so special about that?" teased Peter. "It's not exactly earth-shattering news!"

"Well, she came in a wheelchair and she's called Sally," said Sarah.

"A wheelchair!" shrieked Jemma (who was only six). "Only babies have wheelchairs!"

"That sounds very unkind, Jemma," snapped her mother. "I'm sure there's a very good reason why she came in a wheelchair; perhaps she's had an accident that means she can't walk."

"She looks all right to me," said Sarah, "but it doesn't seem right, somehow."

"That's what the taxi was doing outside school," said Peter. "I wish I had a taxi to bring me to school and take me home every day. Some people have a very easy life."

"I don't know why she's in our class," complained Sarah. "She won't be able to join in things. She won't be able to do PE or run about in the playground; how's she going to get down the steps into the dining room?"

"There's hardly enough room in our classrooms as it is," added Peter, "without having wheelchairs around."

"And how's she going to be able to sit on the carpet for story time?" giggled Jemma.

"Now that's quite enough of that!" snapped Mr Robinson. "I can see she's going to have a tough time if everyone's got the same sort of attitude as you three!"

Nothing more was said about Sally for the next few weeks. Then one day Sarah came home from school quite excited.

"Mum, you know that new girl Sally in the wheelchair?"

"Yes," replied Mrs Robinson, "don't tell me you've got more things to grumble about."

"No, Mum, it's not that at all. Today Sally was my partner to work on the computer. At first I didn't like the idea, but Mum, she's absolutely fantastic! She can do things much quicker than I can, and gets through the programs we're working on in no time. She helped me when I got stuck and is ever so friendly and cheerful. And do you know what? At dinnertime she came to orchestra. And do you know what? She can play the flute and has already done Grade 2 and I've still not got Grade 1!" Sarah hardly paused for breath and her mother couldn't get a word in. "And do you know what?" continued Sarah. "She can swim! She told me she has a special machine for helping her into the water and swims just using her arms. She's got her 25 metres certificate! And do you know what? She is always so cheerful and happy."

"Well, that's quite a change," said her Mum with a smile. "It wasn't long ago that you thought she shouldn't be in your class at all."

"But once you get to know her, Mum, she's like everyone else really," Sarah explained.

"Why not ask her to tea after school one day, and then you'll have a chance to get to know her even better?" said her Mum. "I'll ring her Mum and check that it's all right."

So it was arranged. Sarah was very excited and made some flapjacks as a special treat. Peter and Jemma were not so sure. During tea they talked about all sorts of things, but no one dared to ask anything about the wheelchair, except Jemma. She couldn't hide her curiosity a minute longer.

"Why are you in a wheelchair?" Jemma blurted out with her mouth full of flapjack. Everyone looked at her sharply, and Jemma wondered what she had said wrong.

"I wondered when you were going to ask me that," smiled Sally. "Well, I was born like this. I have never been able to learn to walk. My wheelchair is my legs."

"Didn't it make you feel very unhappy?" asked Sarah nervously.

"Not really," replied Sally. "I just had to learn other ways of doing things. I was sorry that I couldn't run up and down stairs, but it was great fun discovering what I could do in my wheelchair. I just decided that I was going to be like any other girl and be the very best at the things I could do. That's why I like computers, playing the flute and swimming."

"But how do you always seem so cheerful and happy?" insisted Sarah.

"I'm not always happy," Sally replied. "What makes me

very unhappy is when people ignore me and treat me as if I'm like something from another planet."

The three children blushed with shame as they remembered what they had said about Sally.

"Lots of people have helped me," she went on, "people who bothered to understand me and help me do things for myself. That's why I've come to your school – to try to be as normal as possible. I want to be a computer programmer when I grow up. It wasn't easy at first – some children ignored me and that made me very sad, but it's better now."

The three children blushed even more. They talked and talked until Sally's Mum came to collect her. "I think our three have learned quite a lot," Mr Robinson whispered to his wife as they watched Peter, Jemma and Sarah taking it in turns to push Sally's wheelchair to the car.

* * *

Stimulus questions

1. Why do you think Peter, Sarah and Jemma seemed so unkind about Sally at first?
2. What did Sarah mean when she said it didn't seem right for Sally to be at their school?
3. How did Sarah come to change her mind about Sally? What impressed her most? (cheerful)
4. How did Sally explain how she kept so cheerful? (people who understood; being positive)

Thinking time

1. Think of how Sally must have felt on her first day at her new school.
2. Think of someone you know who is in a wheelchair. How do they manage? Could you help?

Prayer

"Lord, help us to understand people who have some disability. Show us how we can help them to live a full life and to share in the things we do. Amen."

FEEDING OF THE FIVE THOUSAND LUKE 9:10-17

THEME: **Sharing**

Amazing things can happen when people share.

"Mum," shouted Dan excitedly, "can I go out with Reuben and Levi?"

"Where are you going to?" asked his mother.

"Oh, just out," he replied.

Dan knew that his mother was very particular whom he went with and where he went. Dan knew that it was all right to go with Reuben and Levi, but to be honest he did not know exactly where they might go, so he couldn't really tell her where they were going!

"Well, you'd better be back for supper – it gets dark early these evenings. Your father doesn't want to have to come looking for you after he's done a hard day's work in the bakery. He's got to be up at the crack of dawn to bake the loaves for people's breakfast."

"We'll be back in time for supper, don't worry," Dan assured her.

"Before you go you'd better take some food with you. You know how hungry you boys get," said his mother.

"But Mother, we want to go now," protested Dan. "There's no time to wait for you to get some food ready."

"Mark my words," she insisted, "you'll be glad you waited. Anyway, you're not going without anything and that's final!"

When his mother said "mark my words" Dan knew there was no point in arguing. He might just as well give in – it was far quicker in the long run. Dan's mother packed him up a picnic of five small loaves, freshly baked by his father that morning, and two fish. Reuben and Levi waited patiently for Dan until at last he was ready.

They discussed what they were going to do. There were quite of lot of things to do in Bethsaida, which was a tiny fishing village on the shore of the Sea of Galilee. Like most boys, they liked messing about in boats, and with some of the loaves that Dan had been made to bring they had plenty of bait for fishing. While they were discussing where to go fishing, Reuben said, "I know what! As I was coming to your house I passed crowds of people going to hear that man Jesus."

"That's a great idea," agreed Levi. "I've heard all sorts of stories about him – that he healed a leper, gave a blind man his sight back and healed the servant of that centurion in Capernaum."

So off they went, following the crowds. They didn't know where they were going, but they soon started to climb up into the hills around. They eventually stopped, but they couldn't see anything because they were at the back of the crowd.

"We won't hear a thing from here," said Dan.

"Don't worry," grinned Reuben, "we're only small; just follow me." They crouched down low and crept between the legs of the crowd until they found themselves in the front row!

"God wants people to be just and kind to one another," Jesus shouted, "not selfish and only looking after themselves. Don't forget, the two main commandments are 'Love God, and love your neighbour as yourself.' How can you claim to love God if you don't love your neighbour? There needs to be a new spirit of sharing. If any of you are ill and need God's blessing, kindly come to the front. God is willing to share his love with all who need him."

There was a general commotion in the crowd. Some had guilty looks on their faces when Jesus talked about being selfish. People who were blind and lame came forward and were healed.

It was getting late and the sun was sinking low when the

disciples came to Jesus and said, "Master, hadn't you better send the crowds away so that they can buy food from the villages around? It will soon be dark and we're miles from any shops."

"You give them something to eat," Jesus said to his disciples.

"We've not got food to feed all these people – there must be 5,000 men and their families."

Jesus looked at them and the people in the front of the crowd. Dan felt sure that Jesus was looking at him with a kindly smile.

"M...M...Master," said Dan shyly, "I've got five small loaves and two fish, if that's any use."

"God is able to do wonderful things when people are willing to share what they have," said Jesus warmly, and he took the picnic that Dan offered.

"Make everyone sit down in groups of 50," Jesus ordered his disciples. "It'll be easier to distribute the food that way."

Then, taking Dan's loaves and fish, Jesus looked up, gave God thanks for the food and broke the loaves. He then gave the food to the disciples to share out among the crowd.

"It's not going to go very far," said Reuben. "There's not enough to feed the first group, even if they only have a tiny piece."

The amazing thing was that there was enough food to go round everyone – and not just a tiny piece, but as much as each person could eat. Dan and the boys didn't know what to make of it. As people ate they said how good the bread tasted.

"I've never tasted bread as good as this before," said one.

"It reminds me of the bread that the village baker in Bethsaida bakes," added another.

"Wasn't it his boy Dan who gave his picnic to Jesus?" said a third. When they had all finished eating, the disciples collected up twelve baskets of broken pieces that were left over.

Slowly the crowds began to melt away, and the three boys ran as fast as they could back to Bethsaida. Dan arrived home quite out of breath. His mother was waiting on the doorstep.

"It's a good thing you've got back," she scolded. "I was just about to send your father to find you. Did you eat your picnic?"

"Yes," Dan replied, "we *all* had more than enough! By the way, I think Father had better bake extra loaves tomorrow; I've a feeling there's going to be a big demand for his bread!"

* * *

Stimulus questions

1. Have you ever been for a picnic? Where? What sort of things do you take to eat?
2. What was it that prompted Dan to offer his picnic to Jesus? Surely he knew there wouldn't be enough for everyone.
3. Have you ever been to a party where everyone brings some item of food? When people share what they have brought, there is usually lots for everyone.
4. Why did Dan suggest that his father should bake extra loaves?
5. What sort of things could you share with someone else?

Thinking time

1. Think of a time when you have been selfish and unwilling to share. How did it make you feel?
2. Think of a time when you shared something you had with someone else. How did you feel?

Prayer

"Lord, forgive us when we are selfish and unwilling to share. Show us how we can bring happiness to other people by sharing with them something we have. Amen."

JEMMA'S AND JULIE'S BIRTHDAY PARTY

THEME: **Sharing**

Good friendships can be made when people share.

Jemma was nearly seven and she had been looking forward to her birthday party for a very long time. In fact, as soon as Christmas was over and all the trimmings and cards and Christmas tree had been packed away for another year, Jemma started to ask, "How long will it be to my birthday?"

"Well," said Peter, her elder brother who was nearly eleven, "it's easy enough even for you to work out!"

"I can't work out months and things," Jemma replied impatiently. "I'm only six – but nearly seven."

"Well, if Christmas Day is on the 25th December and your birthday is on 25th May, you should know how many months you've got to wait," Peter continued, not wanting to give in to Jemma.

"25th January, 25th February, 25th March, 25th April, 25th May," said Jemma quietly to herself, counting on her fingers each time she said a new month. "In five months it will be my birthday," she cried out. "Is that a long time to wait?"

"Well, it's roughly 150 days," said Peter, who didn't like to admit that he wasn't sure which months had 30 days and which had 31 – and then February was always awkward.

"150 days," sighed Jemma. "That's a very, very long time to wait."

Jemma forgot all about her birthday until her mother said one day, "Goodness, it's the 1st May – another month here already."

"May!" shouted Jemma. "That means it's nearly my birthday."

"So it is," agreed her mother. "We shall have to start thinking about your party and sending out invitations."

After that Jemma got very excited. She had already started to think about her cake, and who would come to her party, and what games they would play – and, of course, what present she would like. Then at school one Monday morning, Jemma's teacher, Miss Dexter, gathered the class together on the carpet for "news".

"Who's going to start us off with news this morning?" asked Miss Dexter.

Well, Jemma could hardly contain herself, but she knew that if she were to stand any chance of Miss Dexter asking her to share her news, she would have to sit still, put up her hand and wait. Miss Dexter could see that Jemma was eager to say something from the way she nearly pulled her arm out of its socket!

"Well, Jemma, what's your news today?" Miss Dexter said with a smile.

"It's going to be my birthday on the 25th of this month," Jemma answered proudly. "I'm going to be seven and I'm having a party," she added.

"That's nice. I wonder if anyone else has a birthday in May?" Miss Dexter asked.

A very quiet little girl called Julie, who hardly ever said anything when it was "news", slowly put up her hand.

"So your birthday is in May, too, Julie," said Miss Dexter. "Do you know which day?"

"I think it's the 25th, just like Jemma's," Julie whispered, "and I will be seven as well."

"And I suppose you'll be having a party just like Jemma." Julie looked down at her feet and didn't reply at first. Then she whispered, "No, I've never had a birthday party."

Miss Dexter thought it was better to move on to hear someone else's news, but Jemma noticed that Julie looked very sad.

Julie lived alone with her mother since the family broke up and Mrs Dowty went out to work to pay for all the bills. She tried her hardest to do the best for Julie, but there never seemed time to organise birthday parties. All that she could afford to buy was a small present for Julie to take to other children's birthday parties. What made it quite impossible for Julie to have a party this year was that Mrs Dowty's mother was very ill and she would have to go and look after her. She had arranged that Julie would stay with a neighbour while she was away.

The following week, Jemma's class was having "circle time". Miss Dexter had asked them to think of one thing that each of them would like to do to make someone else happy. The children made all kinds of suggestions. When it came to Jemma's turn, she simply said, "I would share my birthday party with Julie."

Miss Dexter looked quite surprised, but when Mrs Robinson came to collect Jemma after school she told her what Jemma had said. On the way home Jemma told her Mum about circle time and what she had said. "I wonder," thought Mrs Robinson as they walked home. She knew Julie's Mum, so it was easy for her to ring her up and mention Jemma's suggestion. Mrs Dowty was very pleased and said she would mention it to Julie.

The next morning two very excited little girls spent playtime deciding whom they would like to invite to their party, whether they should have one cake to share, or to ask Jemma's Mum to make two. They decided to ask for two.

The party was a great success. They had their favourite games and both girls got quite a lot of presents from the children who came. When it was time to go home the children had two pieces of birthday cake to take home. The best thing was when Mrs

Robinson said, "Oh, by the way, Julie's Mum said she could stay overnight." The girls shouted with excitement.

"I've still not had a birthday party of my very own," grinned Julie, "but this has been much better – and I've made a new friend."

"Amazing things can happen when people share," Mrs Robinson said to herself as she began to clear things up after the party.

* * *

Stimulus questions

1. Can you remember your last birthday? Did you have a party? What did you do?
2. If you had been Jemma or Julie what games would you have at your party?
3. What did Mrs Robinson mean when she said that amazing things happen when people share?

Thinking time

1. Think of how Julie might have felt when Jemma started to tell about her birthday party.
2. Think of how Julie felt when she knew Jemma had asked her to have a shared birthday party.
3. Think of a time when you shared something with someone. How did you feel?

Prayer

"Lord, thank you for all the good things we have. Help us to learn how we can bring happiness to other people by sharing something we have with them. Amen."

THE GOOD SAMARITAN
LUKE 10:25-37

THEME: **My Neighbour**

Anyone who needs help is my neighbour.

"Jacob, what a terrible state you are in," said Judith as she saw her husband arriving home from his journey to Jerusalem. "Whatever happened? You're covered in bandages. I was expecting you back two days ago."

"I'm just lucky to be here at all," groaned Jacob. "Let me come inside and while you're making me a cool drink, I'll tell you everything. It's a most amazing story, but every word is true."

Jacob and Judith lived in Jericho, but Jacob had to go to Jerusalem on business quite often, a journey of about 20 kilometres (15 miles). It was when he was returning to Jericho from Jerusalem that things had gone very, very wrong. He told Judith all about it, while he drank a jar of cool pomegranate juice.

"Well, dear," he began, "I set off from Jerusalem in the afternoon. Knowing how lonely the road is down to Jericho and how people travelling alone have been attacked by bandits and robbers, I tried to join others travelling that way, as I usually do. Unfortunately, I was a bit late setting off and most people had already started. I had to decide whether to stay the night or to risk it on my own. I knew you would worry if I didn't arrive that night, so I set off.

"It was a lovely, quiet afternoon with the late sun just beginning to dip down behind the hills. As I walked further down the road into the valley, it seemed to get dusk quite quickly. I was just rounding a bend when out sprang a gang of about five men, armed with knives and heavy clubs. Before I could cry out for help, they set upon me, dragged me to the ground, and took my bag with all my money. Just to make sure they'd got everything, they stripped off my clothes and gave me a good beating before disappearing into the hills.

"I must have been unconscious for a while, because the next thing I remembered was being unable to move. My leg was badly hurt and my ribs were so sore that they must have been broken. Blood was running down my face and I thought that my end had come. I lay there for some time, unable to move, when I heard footsteps coming up the hill toward Jerusalem. I could tell from his clothes that the man was a priest. I managed to catch his attention by groaning, but when he saw me he crossed to the other side of the road, muttering under his breath, 'I can't stop for him, otherwise I shall be late for the service in the Temple. In any case if I touch him in the state he's in, I shall become impure and not able to do my duty in the Temple.' With that he shuffled off without stopping. I just couldn't believe that a man of God could do that. A little later, I heard more footsteps. This time it was a Levite, one of the Temple servants. Surely he will stop and help, I thought. What better service could he do than help me? He paused briefly and again muttered to himself, 'I'm not falling for this trick. There's sure to be a gang of robbers waiting to pounce on the first person that stops to help.' He quickened his steps and left me.

"I was feeling so thirsty and faint. I didn't think I could last much longer, when again I heard footsteps. I groaned to attract attention, and then almost wished I hadn't! It was a Samaritan riding a donkey. Now, Judith, you know that we Jews don't get on well with the Samaritans. They are sort of half-Jews, and don't keep our religion as they should. I'll admit I've said some pretty awful things about Samaritans, so I didn't expect any help from this one – he might even finish me off altogether, I thought. What I'm going to tell you now is hard to believe, but I swear it's true.

"He came over to me and said, 'What on earth has happened to you? You poor man, you look almost finished. Here, drink this water first. Don't try to move, just stay where you are.' He tore a strip of cloth from his tunic and made it into bandages. He got an oil and wine flask from the donkey, and poured the wine on my wounds to clean them and then poured on soothing oil before bandaging me up. I still couldn't speak, but without asking any questions, he managed to get me on his donkey. The road was bumpy, but the donkey did his best not to shake me about too much. We soon arrived at a roadside inn. He booked a room and soon had me settled on a bed. I can't tell you what a relief it was. He stayed with me all night, giving me drinks of water and checking that the bandages were all right. I didn't get much sleep, but when I awoke, I heard the Samaritan talking to the innkeeper: 'Here's two silver coins. Look after him and if I owe you any more I'll pay you when I return tomorrow.' And with that he was gone. I just didn't have chance to thank him, or ask his name and address, so that I could repay him. The innkeeper didn't know either. The next day I was fit to travel, though still feeling very sore and weak. And here I am."

"It's a miracle you're alive, Jacob," said Judith.

"It's a greater miracle that it was a Samaritan who stopped to help – a complete stranger belonging to a race we just don't get on with," added Jacob.

"It's taught us an important lesson," reflected Judith, "that there are kind and caring people in every race."

"I wish there was some way I could find out who this stranger was. I owe him a big 'thank you'," said Jacob.

"Well, Jacob," said Judith thoughtfully, "you can show your thanks by helping anyone else you meet who needs your help, whatever colour or nationality they may be."

* * *

Stimulus questions

1. Why was Jacob so surprised that the priest and Levite didn't stop to help? Why was he even more surprised that the Samaritan did help?
2. What could the Samaritan have said and done, knowing the Jews and Samaritans did not get on with each other?
3. How did the Samaritan show just how much he cared?
4. Are there people in our world who do not get on well with each other? Who are they?

Thinking time

1. Can you think of an occasion when someone helped you, perhaps when you were lost? How did they show their care for you?

Prayer

"Lord, help us to learn that anyone who needs our help is our neighbour. Help us to show care for them. Amen."

PETER'S BIG SURPRISE

THEME: **My Neighbour**

Even my enemy is my neighbour if he needs my help.

There was only a week to go before half-term and Peter Robinson was looking forward to going with his sisters Sarah and Jemma, and his Mum and Dad, to a caravan by the sea. But Peter was very unhappy. For the past few days he was being troubled by a boy from the local secondary school. It started harmlessly enough, with a bit of name calling. "Tiny kid, tiny kid!" he shouted at Peter as they met on the way home. Peter had learned just to ignore such things, but it got worse. The boy crossed over the road and started pushing Peter into the hedge. "Wait till you start at our school, I'll be on the look-out for you!" he taunted. Peter was really looking forward to starting at the High School in the autumn, but the idea that this boy would be looking out for him worried him. He didn't know what to do. So Peter said nothing to anyone about the bullying. But, of course, his mother and father knew something was wrong.

"Peter, you look as though something is troubling you," his mother said one day when he came home almost in tears after the usual pushing and taunting on his way home.

"Nothing's the matter," snapped Peter, and he dashed straight up to his room.

At tea Peter ate hardly anything. His parents knew something was wrong if he didn't want food.

"Peter," said his father firmly, "there *is* something wrong, so you might just as well tell us what it is now. We don't want to go on holiday next week with you in this state."

Peter realised that he couldn't hide the problem any longer and he really did want to talk about it to someone who would understand and know what to do. So he plucked up courage and told them the whole story.

"What's this boy called and where does he live?" enquired his mother.

"I just know he's called Roy and I've no idea where he lives," Peter replied.

"Look," said his father, "there's only two more days to half-term. Perhaps after the holidays this Roy will get fed up with his silly game. If not, we'll get in touch with the High School. We certainly can't let it go on much longer."

The bullying didn't stop, but Peter put up with it for two more days and then it was half-term. Packing up and getting ready for the caravan almost put the problem out of Peter's mind and he was his usual self again. The Robinsons had just got settled into their caravan when they heard quite a commotion going on outside. Mrs Robinson peeped through the curtains.

"The people next door have just arrived, but they seem to be having trouble getting their caravan open," reported Mrs Robinson. "There's a mother and father and a boy of about twelve." The noise continued and they could hear shouting and banging.

"I'll go and see what the problem is," sighed Mr Robinson. "Perhaps we can help." The children peered through the window to watch their father. Peter gasped with surprise when he saw the boy.

"They've forgotten the caravan key," announced Peter's father when he returned.

"Serves them right," gloated Peter. "I hope it rains and they get wet through!"

"That's not like you, Peter," his mother said sharply. "Whatever's got into you?"

"Well, anyway," continued his father, "I've suggested that

Mrs Dukes and their boy come here for some supper, while Mr Dukes drives home to get the key."

"You've done what?" shrieked Peter. "They deserve to sleep outside and get soaked!"

"I can't understand why you're behaving like this, Peter," snapped his mother. "Just think if we had forgotten our key. Wouldn't you be glad if someone offered to help?"

Peter kept quiet, but was fuming with anger inside. Mrs Dukes came round with their son and introduced themselves to the Robinsons.

"I'm Daphne Dukes and this is our boy Roy," she said.

Mrs Robinson could hardly hide her surprise. She knew exactly why Peter behaved as he did. During supper the two boys glowered at each other and never spoke a word. Mrs Robinson tried to make conversation with Mrs Dukes, but found it hard to hide her feelings. She thought she might find out a few things about the Dukes, especially about Roy.

"Which school does Roy go to?" Mrs Robinson enquired.

"He's finishing his first year at Grantley High School. What about Peter and the girls?"

"They go to King's Road Primary School, but Peter's hoping to start at the High School next term," replied Mrs Robinson, looking hard at Roy.

"I hope he settles in better than Roy did," sighed Mrs Dukes. "He was bullied from the first day. It got so bad he wouldn't go to school, and when he did he got into all kinds of trouble. It's taking us ages to sort out the problem, but the school is being very helpful."

Peter was listening to all this very carefully and noticed that Roy had become quiet and at one point he wiped his face, though he made it look as though he'd got something in his eye.

Mr Dukes finally arrived back with the key to their caravan. Mrs Dukes thanked the Robinsons for the meal and, with Roy looking very ashamed, they went to their caravan.

"So that explains it all," said Mrs Robinson to Peter. "I don't think you'll be having any more trouble from young Roy Dukes."

"Strange how he bullies me, just because he's been bullied," Peter said, quite puzzled.

"Not really," explained Peter's father. "It's his way of reacting to his own problem and trying to get his own back."

While they were at the caravan, the two boys gradually got to know each other better. They talked a lot about school, and Roy told Peter all about the difficult time he had at first.

"I think it was really my own fault," admitted Roy. "You see, I was the biggest boy in my little school and I went to the High School showing off and throwing my weight around. No wonder I got bullied by the others. I'm really sorry that I made your life miserable, Peter."

"That's all right," said Peter. "You've told me a lot that will help me when I go to the High School next term. At least there will be someone I know when I get there."

In the car on the way home, Mr Robinson turned to Peter and with a smile said, "Being a good neighbour to someone in need seems to have solved your other problem too, Peter."

*   *   *

Stimulus questions

1. Is it easy for parents to know when something is wrong? How do they know?
2. Do you think Peter handled the bullying in the right way? What else could he have done?
3. Do you think Peter and Roy became good friends? Could Peter really forgive Roy?

Thinking time

1. Think of a time when someone upset you. Who helped you? Were you able to forgive them?

Prayer

"Lord, help us to learn that our neighbour is anyone who needs our help, whatever they might have done to us. Show us how to forgive them, and to make friends. Amen."

MARY AND MARTHA
LUKE 10:38-42

Kindness

True kindness means thinking of all the needs of others.

Mary and Martha were sisters who lived in a tiny village called
Bethany, which was very near Jerusalem. They were very kind
sisters and got on well together, but they were totally different
from each other. Martha was very practical and seemed to
think of everything that needed doing. She was the one who
remembered to do the shopping – and kept a careful list of all
they needed. She knew which day the fishmonger came round
with fresh fish, and when to go to the baker's to get the fresh-
est loaves. She liked to have meals ready at exactly the same
time each day – and expected everyone to be punctual.

Mary was not like this at all. She was just as kind as
Martha and didn't mind doing her share of the work, but she
was much more "laid-back" than Martha. Mary was rather
more interested in the people that had been invited to tea than
fussing about being sure that everything was on the table just
at the right time. She was always keen to ask how people were
and what sort of day they had had. She was very concerned if
someone was not feeling too well. She always had time to listen
to someone who had a good story to tell, or who had heard a bit
of gossip. People felt welcome and important. When they came
to Martha's and Mary's home they went to Mary for a chat,
while Martha fussed around getting things ready.

Well, Martha and Mary heard that Jesus was coming to
Jerusalem, which was only a little distance from their house in
Bethany. They were afraid of what might happen if he stayed in

Jerusalem. There were lots of people there who wanted to get rid of him altogether.

"What are we going to do, Mary?" asked Martha anxiously. "There's bound to be trouble if Jesus stays in Jerusalem."

"Why don't we ask him to stay with us here?" replied Mary.

"Oh! I'm not sure that I could manage that. Think of all the things we would have to do – getting the spare room ready, cleaning the house from top to bottom, ordering extra food. And how do we know what he likes to eat?" said Martha with a very worried look on her face.

"I'm sure he would be very grateful to stay in our simple home and not expect a lot of extras," Mary replied. "Wouldn't it be marvellous to have him stay here? We could listen to all he had to say without being hassled by all the crowds that usually follow him around."

"Well, if you're sure it will be all right," Martha said finally, "it really would be good to offer him a safe place to stay."

So it was agreed. From that very moment until the day Jesus arrived, Martha was working frantically. She scrubbed and cleaned, dusted and polished, washed and ironed – you really would have thought that the king was coming to stay. Mary did what she could to help, but wondered if Martha would be in any fit state to make Jesus feel welcome.

The day came when Jesus arrived. He had had a long journey and all he really wanted was a quiet place to rest. Mary noticed this and would have taken him straight to his room, but Martha took over. She had been working all day to get an enormous meal ready for him. She had timed everything so that it was ready by sunset. The chicken was cooked and all the vegetables just ready to eat. So as soon as Jesus arrived he was whisked to the table and Martha started serving dinner. She showed her kindness by the amount of food she served – enough to feed three or four people. Jesus looked at all the food, but couldn't say that he would prefer something simple. Mary ate with Jesus, but Martha was fussing so much that she didn't sit down herself. She was equally quick to clear everything away after the meal. Dishes and pots and pans were all taken to the kitchen and Martha started the washing-up. She was getting more and more worked up.

Mary took Jesus out on the verandah and sat and listened to what he had to say. He explained why he had come to Jerusalem and that he expected there would be trouble. Many had turned against him because they were jealous of the way he had attracted crowds of people. Mary listened patiently, only occasionally asking a question. She was fascinated by all that he had to say. Jesus found it easy to talk to Mary – she really listened. He was concerned about what might happen to him and needed someone to talk things over with. Mary was just the right person.

"It's all right you just sitting there chatting," burst in Martha, "leaving me all the work to do. Sitting talking won't get things cleared away. Jesus, we are so glad to have you stay with us, but there are lots of extra things to do – you don't seem to care that my sister has left me to do the work by myself!"

It wasn't usual for Martha to lose her temper in this way, but she had been rushing around for so long to get things just right for Jesus that it had all become too much for her. Mary looked at Jesus and blushed with embarrassment. She just didn't know what to say.

"Martha," Jesus said in a calm and kindly voice, "you've got worried and upset about so many things and I really am grateful for all the work you have done for me, but all I really needed was a place where I could be quiet and feel safe among friends. Mary has given me these things. She noticed I was tired after my journey. She saw that I was anxious about the danger in Jerusalem. But more than anything she sat down quietly and listened to what I had to say. I'm not going to stop her." Martha looked quite ashamed.

"Why don't you come and sit down quietly with us for a while," said Jesus, "and then we'll all do the washing-up?"

Martha did just that and enjoyed listening along with Mary. The washing-up took the three of them no time at all.

* * *

Stimulus questions

1. The two sisters were very different. Which of them was more important? Which do you think you would like better? Was Mary just being lazy and leaving everything to Martha?
2. Have you ever had anyone really important to stay with you? What if you had a letter from Buckingham Palace to say that the Queen was visiting your town and wanted to come and have tea with you? How would your mother react? What sort of things would she want to do before the Queen came?
3. What if you only had someone like a "Martha"? Would the Queen feel welcome? What sort of things would a "Mary" be concerned about?

Thinking time

1. Just imagine that someone really important was going to stay with you. What sort of "Martha" things would need doing?
2. What sort of "Mary" things would make the person feel really welcome?

Prayer

"Lord, when we try to be kind to other people, help us to think about them and how they feel and not just what we want to do for them. Amen."

MR AND MRS ROBINSON CREATE A GOOD IMPRESSION!

THEME: **Kindness**

True kindness means putting other people first.

"Anything interesting happened at work today, Steve?" asked Kate Robinson as she served the evening meal.

"I'll say there was," replied Steve Robinson. "A notice went up telling us who our new boss is going to be."

"Well, you've waited long enough to find out. Is it someone from your firm?"

"No, a complete stranger," explained Mr Robinson. "He's called Vikesh Patel. They say he's very good, but strict on discipline and standards. Moves down here with his family next month."

"I hope they settle in easily, especially if they have children. Perhaps they'll go to the same school as Peter, Sarah and Jemma. Our three are good at making new friends," said Mrs Robinson.

"What's more important," said Mr Robinson, "is that I create a good impression. Unusual name – but it's what he's really like that matters. I need to keep in with him – if I play my cards right he could make me his deputy. What if we invite him and his wife to dinner as soon as they move? It's important to get in first before any others in the office get the same idea."

So it was arranged. Vikesh Patel and his wife, Mazia, were invited to dinner with the Robinsons. Mr and Mrs Robinson had taken ages planning what they should have to eat.

"It's got to be something special," said Mr Robinson. "We've got to create a good impression!"

"What about this one for starters?" said Mrs Robinson, studying her Delia Smith cookbook. "Hot and Sour Pickled Prawns – it says you can prepare it the day before and have it ready to serve."

"And what about this for the main course?" added Mr Robinson excitedly. "Pork Saltimbocca. It sounds very exotic – they're bound to notice that we've created a good impression."

"This sounds good for pudding," said Mrs Robinson. "Terrine of Summer Fruits. It's made with strawberries, raspberries and blackcurrants soaked in wine and set with gelatine."

"Talking of wine," added Mr Robinson, "I'll get a bottle of expensive wine and some champagne for a welcome toast. It's going to cost us a fortune but we've got to create a good impression!"

Mrs Robinson made a special effort to make sure the house was clean and tidy. The three children were given strict orders to clear away all their things from the lounge and Mr Robinson even cut the front lawn. When the day arrived, Peter, Sarah and Jemma were given tea early and the two younger ones sent to bed, though Peter was allowed to read for half an hour before turning off his light. Mrs Robinson had been to the hairdressers and got her hair styled, and Mr Robinson had bought a new shirt and tie for the occasion. "Got to create a good impression," he kept saying as they got ready. At 7.30 pm the doorbell rang. "That'll be them," Mr Robinson said excitedly, and ran downstairs to open the door.

"Hello, Mr and Mrs Patel," he said cheerily, "do come in – I hope the traffic wasn't too busy. This is my wife Kate." They all shook hands.

"Please, Steve, it's not Mr and Mrs Patel tonight," said Mr Patel. "I'm Vikesh and this is my wife Mazia. We're very pleased to meet you. It is kind of you to invite us to dinner."

"We seem to have created a good impression straightaway," Mr Robinson whispered to his wife as they went into the lounge.

"Would you like a drink before dinner?" Mr Robinson asked. "I've got some rather special wine."

"Thank you, but we would prefer orange juice, if you don't mind," replied Mr Patel.

"Of course," said Mr Robinson, wondering if they had any orange juice in the house.

After the drink and friendly chat, Mr Robinson showed them into the dining room while Mrs Robinson got things organised in the kitchen. She proudly presented the first course.

"Hot and Sour Pickled Prawns," she announced with a flourish.

Mr and Mrs Patel looked at each other uncertainly. While the hosts ate eagerly, they noticed that their guests ate very little, and spent most of the time stirring the food around. Mrs Robinson cleared the plates, noticing that the Patels had hardly eaten anything. She thought that perhaps they didn't like prawns, and felt more confident when she brought in the Pork Saltimbocca.

"It's a new dish I've discovered," she announced proudly. "Pork with Parma ham, fresh sage leaves and olives, cooked in the finest olive oil."

But however much she enthused about the food, the Patels did not seem impressed. They rather seemed embarrassed and could only manage a faint smile. Again they stirred the food around and managed to eat a few olives. They didn't eat any of the pork. Mr Robinson was quite worried. Was the food burned or not cooked properly? His tasted perfectly all right. "Not creating much of an impression on them," he thought to himself. "I wonder if they're feeling ill?" He looked at his wife and she looked at him. "What could be the matter?" she thought. Again the plates were cleared away. "At least the pudding should be all right," Mrs Robinson sighed to herself as she brought in the Terrine of Summer Fruits. However, things were not much better. Mr and Mrs Patel carefully scooped the fruit away from the gelatine, which they left on the side of their plates. Mr Robinson was getting very anxious. After dinner the Patels went back to the lounge while Mr Robinson joined his wife in the kitchen.

"What's gone wrong?" he whispered loudly. "They've hardly eaten a thing – just think of all the time and money we've spent trying to impress them."

"I know," agreed Mrs Robinson, "they look so embarrassed – I wonder what's wrong?"

While they were drinking coffee and trying to make conversation, Mr Patel suddenly said, "Look, you must think that we are very rude. You kindly invite us to dinner and we have not been able to eat the beautiful food you have prepared for us. Please forgive us..."

"Well, we couldn't help noticing," said Mrs Robinson. "Was there something wrong with it?"

"We really have tried our best," added Mr Robinson, knowing that he had lost all hope of impressing them. How could he hope to be Mr Patel's deputy now?

"Let me explain," hastened Mr Patel. "You see, my wife and I are Hindus and we were brought up to be strict vegetarians. Eating meat of any kind really makes us feel ill."

"Oh! We're terribly sorry," said Mrs Robinson anxiously. "That explains why you didn't eat the prawns or the pork." She knew that the gelatine in the pudding was made from animal bones, but didn't like to say so.

"We really should have told you," said Mrs Patel apologetically, "but we hardly knew you and didn't want to upset you. We just hoped there would be things we could eat."

After the Patels had gone, Mr Robinson turned to his wife and said, "That's what happens when you try to impress people without really thinking about *them* and what *they* would like."

* * *

Stimulus questions

1. Do you think Mr and Mrs Robinson were really trying to be kind to the Patels?
2. What things did they do to try to impress them? Did they want to be friends, or something else?
3. Should the Patels have said they were vegetarians at the beginning?
4. Do you think that Mr Robinson would get promotion to be Mr Patel's deputy? Why?
5. How could Mr Robinson really impress Mr Patel?

Thinking time

1. If you were Mr or Mrs Robinson, think of the things you would do to make Mr and Mrs Patel feel welcome.
2. How could Peter, Sarah and Jemma help the Patel children?

Prayer

"Lord, when we try to be kind to other people, help us to think about their needs and not just what we can do to impress them. Amen."

THE PRODIGAL SON
LUKE 15:11-32

THEME: **Forgiveness**

Forgiveness means forgetting the past.

Jacob had two sons, Dan and Ben. Though Dan was only a little older than Ben, they were totally different people. Dan was rather quiet, not exactly miserable, but he always looked slightly anxious. Ben, however, was always bright and cheerful and ready for a joke and a bit of fun. They both worked on their father's farm.

"I don't think I want to stick at home for ever," said Ben. "Working on Father's farm is all right, but there must be more to life than this. I want a bit of excitement."

"Well," said Dan, in a mournful voice, "Father rather depends on us. It's a steady job. We know exactly what to do and Father does give us a decent wage."

"That's just the trouble," broke in Ben. "It's so boring; day in, day out, doing the same things. There must be a lot more fun out there, but we're stuck on the farm, with no chance of ever getting away to see the big world. I'm not going to stick it any longer!"

With that, Ben plucked up courage and went to his father.

"Father," he said, "I expect that when you die you will leave the farm to me and Dan. By that time we might be quite old ourselves. I'd like the chance to enjoy myself a bit while I'm young. Please can I have my share of your money now, so that I can go off and enjoy myself?"

"But Ben," protested his father, "that hardly seems fair to Dan – leaving him alone to work on the farm."

"It is fair," argued Ben. "If I have my share now, then everything that is left will be Dan's."

After a great deal of arguing, Ben's father reluctantly agreed and gave Ben his share of the money. Within a week Ben had made plans to set off to see the world. He said goodbye to his father and Dan and off he went.

Ben thought that from now on life was going to be wonderful, and for a time it was. He set off to a distant country where he'd heard that life was full of thrills and excitement. He stayed at the best hotels, eating the most expensive food, and in no time at all he had lots of friends. He was never without friends, especially when they realised that he had plenty of money. They helped him to spend it on the finest clothes, wining and dining in the most expensive restaurants. Ben, of course, always picked up the bill.

This went on for some months, until one day Ben reckoned up how much money he had got left. The answer was not very much at all. "But I've got plenty of friends," he said. "They'll see me right." But when word got round that Ben had no money, his friends seemed to disappear. He tried calling on them, but they were either "not at home" or "too busy". Some even pretended that they didn't know him at all! What made it worse was that there was a famine and food was very difficult to get, even if you had plenty of money, which Ben hadn't. He tried to get a job, but the only one he could find was feeding pigs. He was so hungry that he was even tempted to eat the swill he fed to the pigs. None of his so-called "friends" were anywhere to be found.

One day, having finished feeding the pigs, he thought to himself, "The farm workers on my father's farm have a much better time than I'm having. At least they have plenty of food to eat, and I'm starving." Then he made the biggest decision in his life, though it wasn't an easy one to make. "I will set off and go back home," he said to himself, "and I will say to father, 'Father, I've been the biggest fool imaginable. I've caused you great worry and upset, and I'm not fit to be your son any more. I am truly sorry for the stupid things I've done, but I've learned my lesson. Will you give me a job on the farm as an ordinary farm worker?"' It was such a difficult decision to make. He thought of all the things his father might say, like telling him that he had had his chance and it was no good coming back when things had gone wrong. More than once he turned back, but realised that he owed it to his father to let him know that he was still alive.

It was a warm sunny afternoon and Jacob was out in the fields. Whatever he was doing on the farm, there was always one thing on his mind. Never a day passed without him thinking, "I wonder how Ben's getting on?" He looked up and saw a distant figure walking towards the farm. He had always hoped that one day he would look up and see Ben coming home, so he quickly put this idea from his mind. "Perhaps it's a salesman coming to sell me some seed," he thought. But as the figure got nearer, he became so excited. "It is Ben," he cried out. "I can tell from the way he walks!" He ran to Ben, threw his arms round him and hugged and kissed him.

"I'm sorry, Dad, for all I've done," said Ben, struggling to hold back his tears. "I'm not fit to be your son – will you forgive me? Please can I have a job on the farm to pay you back?"

His father hardly heard a word. He turned to one of his servants and said, "Quick! Go and get the finest outfit of clothes and the best pair of sandals – and get that golden ring in my drawer. Tell the cook to get the best meal ready – we're going to have a party! My son was as good as dead and he is alive and well! I thought I'd lost him for ever, but here he is!" And he hugged him all over again. When Dan heard all the commotion he asked what it was all about.

"Your brother's back," a servant yelled with delight.

"Oh, him!" groaned Dan angrily. "He took Father's money and wasted it all, leaving me to work like a slave on the farm.

Then as soon as he comes back Father treats him like a prince. Well, I'm not going to any party. I've not got anything to be pleased about."

They gave Ben a great welcome-home party. Everyone was glad to see him back, except Dan. It took a long, long time before the two brothers became real friends again.

* * *

Stimulus questions

1. Brothers and sisters are often very different from each other. Is that the same in your family? In what way?
2. What were the good qualities in Ben and Dan?
3. If you had been Ben's father, would you have given him his share of the money?
4. Have you ever found you suddenly had lots of friends when you had something special – sweets to share, or a new game to play?
5. Was Ben's father right to make such a fuss about him?
6. What do you think of Dan's attitude? Was he right?

Thinking time

1. Think of a time when you did something wrong that you were sorry about. How hard was it to say "sorry"? What happened when you did say "sorry"?

Prayer

"Lord, when someone does something wrong to us and then they are really sorry, give us the strength to forgive them and behave as if it had never happened. Amen."

PETER RUNS AWAY FROM HOME

THEME: **Forgiveness**

Forgiveness means making a new start.

Peter Robinson didn't really mind having two younger sisters, but he did sometimes wish that Sarah, who was eight, and three years younger than he was, had been a boy. Six-year-old Jemma was always good fun, but too little to be much good at football, even if she had been a boy. What really bothered Peter was that his parents always seemed to take Sarah's side. If they were having a friendly scrap, his mother would say, "Now Peter, don't be too rough; remember Sarah is much younger than you. It's time you grew up and started acting your age. Your Grandad started work soon after he was twelve." Then, when Peter started behaving as a grown-up and asked if he could go to a disco in town with his friends, what did his father say? "A disco in town at your age? You're only a child, Peter!" He just couldn't win. First, he was grumbled at for acting like a child and then he was told off for wanting to be grown-up. If life was going to be like this from now on, it wasn't going to be much fun.

Things came to a head one Friday evening when Peter had asked if he could have a new pair of Nike trainers costing £65, because all the boys in his class, well – nearly all, had got some. His father, who had had a very stressful week at work, lost his temper. "What? £65 just like that! You must think that money grows on trees! I'm not flogging my guts out all week to provide you with the latest fashion in trainers!" And that was the end of that. Peter went up to his room and thought to himself, "I just seem to be in the way here; always in trouble – never get anything right. There's always money whenever Sarah wants new clothes. I shall be better off on my own, then Sarah and Jemma can have the little bit of money they spend on me." Poor Peter really did feel sorry for himself. But he was determined. He got out the bag he kept his swimming things in, and stuffed in a few clothes with his swimming things on top. He collected together what cash he had saved, plus the £10 his Grandma had given him on a recent visit.

When Peter came down for breakfast the next day, there were only Sarah and Jemma in the kitchen.

"Where are Mum and Dad?" he asked.

"They've gone to town early to avoid the rush," replied Sarah, "but they said you had to stay with us till they got back. They said they wouldn't be long."

"Did they?" said Peter defiantly. "Well, that's too bad, because I'm going out! If they want to know where I've gone, as they usually do, tell them I've gone swimming with Clive."

With that he slung his bag over his shoulder and walked out.

"Freedom at last," he thought, as he made his way to the bus stop. When he got to town, he kept a careful watch in case he should meet his parents, but felt safe in heading straight for McDonalds – his parents never went there. After a double burger, large fries and coke, he wandered around until he came to Dixons. One of the things he had wanted for some time, but was always given the "money doesn't grow on trees" story, was a Nintendo Game Cube. He didn't have to ask anyone if he could have one now. He walked in, decided he had enough money, and bought it. When the salesman said, "A birthday present, is it?" Peter just smiled. By now he was feeling tired but very pleased with himself. Passing the multiplex cinema, he spotted a film called *The Scorpion King*, but it had a 12 certificate. "That's no problem," he thought, and stretching himself as tall as he could and trying to speak in a deep voice, he bought a ticket and in he went. Life felt very good.

Back at home, Mr and Mrs Robinson were not feeling so good. Where could Peter be? It wasn't like him to miss meals, and he had missed lunch and tea. They rang Clive's parents, but Clive hadn't gone swimming. They rang his other friends, but no one had seen Peter. "Perhaps he's gone to Grandma's," thought Mrs Robinson. "I'll give her a ring."

"No, dear, Peter's not been here," said Grandma with a note of anxiety in her voice. "He did seem rather unhappy last time we came over. Steve does seem hard on him at times. I hope he's all right – you know what boys are like when they're growing up."

Mr and Mrs Robinson talked over what Grandma had said and couldn't help but agree with her.

When Peter came out of the cinema, it was dark and raining and all the shops were closed. He had spent nearly all his money and began to feel quite miserable. He had had time to think. The Nintendo Game Cube, which he had wanted so badly, wasn't much good now and he was hungry again. If he were at home now, he would have had a good meal and be watching the football results with his Dad. But he couldn't very well go home now, after what he had done. Then he had an idea. His grandparents always seemed to understand him and though they were old and not very exciting, they were always ready to listen to him and encourage him. Perhaps they could help. He had just enough money for the bus fare, and timidly rang the doorbell.

"Peter, how lovely to see you," said his Grandad. "Come in! You look hungry to me."

Grandma smiled with relief at seeing him and set about getting him some food. That was the really good thing about his grandparents – they treated him as if they knew what it was like to be a boy of eleven, nearly twelve. It wasn't long before Peter told them the whole story and what had led up to his running away.

"But how can I go home now, Grandma?" he said. "Can't I stay with you and Grandad?"

"You know you can stay with us any time, Peter," his Grandma replied, "but I think that it would be best if you let Grandad take you home – I know your Mum and Dad are worried."

"But what will they do to me?" he pleaded.

"I think they will be so glad to see you that you need not worry. Why not tell them everything you've told us? Then ask your Dad what it was like for him when he was nearly twelve."

So Peter went home and much to his surprise, his parents listened to his story.

"I'm sorry I've caused you so much worry," he said. "Will you be able to forgive me?"

"You're forgiven already, Peter," his Dad said, "and from now on we had better listen more carefully to what you're trying to tell us."

"By the way, Dad," added Peter, "Grandma said I was to ask you what it was like when you were nearly twelve. What did she mean?"

"It might just mean that she remembers when I did a very similar thing!" his father said.

* * *

Stimulus questions

1. Why do you think Peter was having such difficulty at home? Can you understand his feelings?
2. Were his parents wrong not to give him everything he wanted? What had he still to learn?

3. Why do you think his grandparents seemed to find it easier to understand him than his parents?
4. What lessons did both Peter and his parents learn from his adventure?
5. Why did Grandma tell Peter to ask his Dad what it was like when he was twelve?

Thinking time

1. Think of a time when you demanded things from your parents. What was their answer? Were they being unkind?
2. Think of someone you could turn to when you have problems like Peter.

Prayer

"Lord, when we do things that cause people to worry, give us courage to say we are sorry, and the determination to make a fresh start. Amen."

THE RICH YOUNG RULER
LUKE 18:18-25

THEME: **Possessions**
Money and power cannot buy the best things in life.

Nathan sat back in his chair and basked in the warm sun. He thought how well he had done for himself. Still only a young man, he was the richest person in town and had more power and authority than people twice his age – and when it came to good looks, there was no one to match him. He'd got everything – fine house, stable full of the fastest horses, and he owned more than 20 farms. He took holidays whenever he wanted, always wore the most expensive clothes and had the best wine cellar for miles. He was quite generous and often had parties to which he invited the whole village.

Yet there was something that troubled him. He loved God and tried to serve him, but he wasn't sure that he'd done enough to be certain of having a place in heaven. Anything he wanted he just bought, however much it cost. But he didn't know what he had to do to get a place in heaven.

While he was thinking about this, his farm manager rushed in out of breath.

"I'm sorry I'm late, master," he said, "but there's such a crowd around that new teacher from Nazareth that I couldn't get through. I've never seen such crowds."

"Who is this teacher?" enquired Nathan.

"He's called Jesus and has been doing some amazing things – healing lepers and blind people and saying some astonishing things about the kingdom of heaven. It's all upside down to me; he reckons that the first shall be last and the last first, and that the greatest must be a servant to everyone else! I really can't understand that."

The farm manager went off to catch up with his work and left Nathan thinking. "Is this Jesus the person who can answer my question?" he thought, and without waiting any longer he set off into town to find him.

He waited until the crowds had gone away, and then went up to Jesus.

"Teacher, what must I do to be sure of getting into the kingdom of heaven?" he said with real determination.

"Well," replied Jesus, "you must know the commandments – do not steal, do not lie, do not murder, do not commit adultery, and honour your father and mother."

Nathan thought for a while. He'd never had to steal because he could always buy what he wanted; he had enough power to get his own way without even having to think about lying or murdering anyone; his good looks ensured that he never had trouble finding girlfriends – and he was taking very good care of his elderly parents.

"Well, if that's all, there's no problem," he said looking very pleased with himself. "I've kept all these since I was a boy."

Nathan was just about to set off for home when Jesus caught hold of the sleeve of his very expensive cloak. "Er, there is just one thing more you need to do…" said Jesus.

Before Jesus could finish, Nathan said, "Well, I suppose I could dig a new well for the village and save them from having to walk so far for water. I could easily do that with the extra money I got from selling a farm last week."

Jesus smiled and shook his head. "That's not what I mean," he said.

"All right," interrupted Nathan, "I'll build a new syna- gogue for the village – that's bound to please God, and they'll be able to put a silver plate up saying that I gave the money."

Jesus smiled and shook his head again. "That's not what I mean either," he said.

"Oh! I think I see what you're getting at," said Nathan rather impatiently. "I'll give you a very generous donation to help with the good work you are doing."

Jesus shook his head vigorously and said, "That's certainly not what I mean!"

Nathan look puzzled. "Then what do you mean?" he said earnestly.

Jesus looked straight at him and thought what a fine young man he was. "There's just one more thing. Sell all that you have and give the money to the poor!"

Nathan froze. It was as if he had been hit by a thunderbolt. "W – w – what?" he trembled. "I've got such a lot; I can't give it all away. Doesn't God like rich people?"

"Nathan," said Jesus tenderly, "God loves everybody, even rich people. But your money and power have made you very proud. Because you can buy anything you want, you think that you can buy God. In God's kingdom the greatest people are those who are willing to be servants to others. You'll find it very hard to be like this, if you go on thinking your money and power can get you everything. The best way for you to learn to be a servant is to give away your money."

Nathan listened carefully. He understood what Jesus meant. He looked straight at Jesus for a few seconds longer, and then with his head down and his shoulders drooping he slowly walked away. He had never felt so sad in all his life.

* * *

Stimulus questions

1. Do you think the rich young man went and sold all he had and gave the money to the poor? What makes you think that?
2. What would you do if you won £1 million? Would it change your life? How?

3. What do you think Jesus meant when he said "the first shall be last, and the last first" and "the greatest must be a servant"?
4. What really valuable things are there that money cannot buy?

Thinking time

1. Think of the things you would buy with £1 million.
2. Think of all the things that are really worth having, that you cannot buy with money.

Prayer

"Lord, thank you for giving us so much. Help us to use what we have to help others who are less fortunate than we are. Amen."

MOUNTAIN BIKE MANIA

THEME: **Possessions**

True friendship is more valuable than anything money can buy.

Peter Robinson had lots of friends at school, but there were four boys that he counted as his special friends – John, David, Clive and Stephen. They played football together, belonged to the same school clubs and were looking forward to going on the Year 6 residential visit to the Isle of Wight later in the year. Being a gang of five was ideal when they played football, which they did every lunchtime. One in goal and two-a-side. It gave them plenty of passing practice as well as shooting at the goal.

One wet lunchtime, when there was no point in rushing their packed lunches, John suddenly said, quite out of the blue, "What would make you the happiest person in the world?" The others stopped munching sandwiches and crunching crisps and looked at each other. You could almost read on their faces what they were thinking: "There he goes again with his fanciful questions."

Getting no immediate response from anyone, John finally said, "Well, I know what would make me happy – if Dad would make his mind up about taking us to Florida next summer – I've heard that Disney World is great."

Peter, David and Clive thought they might as well join in John's little game and without much hesitation all agreed that they would settle for their favourite team's new football strip.

"You're quiet, Stephen, what about you?" demanded John. They were such good friends that they didn't like anyone being missed out.

Stephen leaned back in his chair, looked at the ceiling and

with a broad grin that stretched from ear to ear said, "Well, I know what I'd choose – and I'm getting one next week!"

"What's that?" they all exclaimed, hardly able to contain their excitement.

"One of those new aluminium-framed mountain bikes with 24 gears," beamed Stephen proudly, "and it costs more than £200." John's question had given him the perfect opportunity to make this proud announcement.

"Wow!" they shouted all together. "And it's not even his birthday," added David.

Sure enough, next week Stephen got his "super de luxe" 24-gear mountain bike. The other four didn't see so much of Stephen from that time. He'd whizz past them without stopping, giving them a look that told them he was now in quite a different league from them. Talking of "leagues", he no longer bothered to play football with them.

"He's really messed things up," moaned Clive. "If we have one in goal we can't have teams of two any more."

"That's not the worst thing," added Peter thoughtfully. "Since he got that mountain bike he's become different somehow."

"What do you mean?" John asked.

"Well," explained Peter, " it's not just the football; he doesn't seem to bother with us any more. He walks past with that superior look on his face as if because he's got this posh bike he's better than we are. Just because his parents can afford to buy him all the latest crazes makes him think he's somebody special. When we were all together he was such good fun. He'd do anything to help if you were stuck with something and always kept you feeling cheerful. He's just changed."

The others all agreed with Peter, but didn't know what they could do to help Stephen see how he was spoiling their friendship.

For the next three weeks the situation got worse. It was almost as if Stephen had never been friends with any of them. Then one Saturday morning Clive was coming out of the paper shop with his football magazine, when he was sure he saw Stephen across the road – walking! Where was his beloved bike?

When the four met in the afternoon to play football, David broke the news.

"I heard my Mum on the phone to Stephen's Mum and she said that Stephen's bike had been stolen on Friday night from outside the chip shop. They'd reported it to the police who would make enquiries but they didn't give much hope of finding it."

They'd just started playing their new football game, "every man for himself", when they caught sight of Stephen just behind the hedge.

"He looks a bit miserable," said Peter to the others. "Shall we ask him if he wants to join in?"

"I'm not keen, after what he's been like," argued John. The others agreed with him about this, but Stephen looked so pathetic on his own that they decided to ask him.

"At least we shall be able to play our two-a-side game, like we used to," said Peter generously.

Stephen was glad to join in. They had a good game in the circumstances, but nobody said anything about the bike. It was when they were strolling off the field that Stephen broke the silence. "Thanks for asking me to play," he said, with a quiver in his voice. "I'm sorry I've lost my bike, but I'm even more sorry that I've lost my mates. I know it didn't look like it, but riding that bike on my own wasn't half as good as messing about with you lot. Having my bike stolen has really taught me a lesson I hope I shall never forget – you can't get decent friends as easily as you can buy a new bike."

The other four didn't know what to say. Perhaps it wasn't the time for saying anything. After a while they all gave Stephen a healthy thump and then all five tore away, shouting and laughing at the top of their voices.

Two weeks later the police recovered Stephen's bike. They found it in a ditch in the next village. Stephen was glad to have it back, but they still played "one in goal and two-a-side" as they always had done.

* * *

Stimulus questions

1. How did Stephen change when he got his new mountain bike?
2. How did it spoil his friendship with the others?
3. What lessons did Stephen learn from losing his mountain bike?
4. What would make you the happiest person in the world? Why?
5. What things are there about your friends that you couldn't buy with money?

Thinking time

1. Think of your friends – the things you do together; how you stick up for each other; how lonely you would be without them.
2. Think of the good things about friends that money couldn't buy.

Prayer

"Lord, we thank you for our friends. When we spoil a friendship give us courage to put it right. Teach us that there are many valuable things in life that money cannot buy. Amen."

ZACCHAEUS
LUKE 19:1-10

THEME: **Making a Fresh Start**

Everybody needs the opportunity to make a fresh start.

Zacchaeus was a chief tax collector, who lived in Jericho, which was only a few miles from Jerusalem. He was very, very rich, perhaps the richest man in town. He had everything that money could buy – a big house, beautiful furniture, plenty of servants, all the latest fashions in clothes and a new horse every year!

But, strange as it may seem, Zacchaeus was very, very unhappy. There were two things that made him unhappy – he had no friends and he was very little! He knew he couldn't do anything about his size, but he did sometimes look at the Roman soldiers and wished he were as tall as they were. All his money couldn't do anything to alter his size! But you would have thought that with all his money he surely would have had plenty of friends, even if it were only his money they wanted him for. But Zacchaeus had no friends at all.

The reason why Zacchaeus had no friends was because of the way that he got his money. He was a tax collector, but not just an ordinary tax collector; he was a chief tax collector. The way he got rich was by overcharging people for the amount of tax they owed. He would suddenly increase taxes without giving any real reason and people were afraid not to pay lest the Romans put them in jail. It made no difference whether people were rich or poor. Rich people had to pay large sums of money in taxes to keep out of trouble, and the very poor people found that when they had paid their taxes to Zacchaeus they had very little left to live on. No wonder he had no friends at all. But

Zacchaeus was not completely without feelings. He enjoyed making lots of money and having all the things that money could buy, but he did think of the poor people who could hardly buy a loaf of bread after they had paid their taxes. But what could he do about it? Deep down in his heart he really longed for a way of making a completely fresh start to his life.

One day Zacchaeus found out that Jesus was passing through Jericho on his way to Jerusalem. Now he had heard that Jesus had shown kindness to people who had made a mess of their lives and who were truly sorry and wanted to make a fresh start. He had helped another tax collector called Matthew do this – in fact, Matthew had become one of his twelve disciples. If only Zacchaeus could talk to Jesus, perhaps he could make a new beginning.

He went into town and found crowds of people lining the road where Jesus was to pass. Of course, his other problem, being so small, meant that he couldn't see over the heads of the people in front. Nobody was willing to let him push his way forward. However, he noticed a huge sycamore-fig tree with branches that were overhanging the road. "This gives me an idea," he thought. He quietly climbed up the tree and hid himself in the branches. "With any luck," he said to himself, "Jesus will pass underneath." That is exactly what happened. The very unusual thing was that although Zacchaeus was well hidden in the branches, Jesus stopped under the tree and said, "Zacchaeus, what are you doing up there? Come down at once; I'd like to stay at your house today!" Well, you can imagine how thrilled Zacchaeus was – he nearly fell out of the tree in his haste to get down.

"Thank you, Lord, I shall be very pleased to welcome you into my house." No one had ever wanted to come to Zacchaeus' house before. The people muttered, "He's gone to stay with that 'wicked sinner' who robs us of our money!" Zacchaeus was so pleased that Jesus was prepared to give him a fresh start and be his friend, that he said, in front of all the people, "Thank you for giving me a fresh start in life. To prove that I'm going to be a totally different person from now on, I want to give half of my money to the poor and if anyone can show that I have cheated them then I will repay him four times as much."

The crowds were amazed to be hearing such things. Jesus said, "Zacchaeus, today you have made a new beginning to your life." Turning to the crowds Jesus said, "You have heard what Zacchaeus has promised to do. I trust that you will give him another chance. God cares for him just as much as any of you. It is to help people who have lost their way that I have come."

Jesus stayed with Zacchaeus that day, and he had lots of questions to ask Jesus about beginning a new life. Jesus told him that it wouldn't be easy. Everyone in Jericho knew what he had been like and it would take a long time for them to learn to trust him.

The next day Jesus had to leave Jericho to make his way to Jerusalem. As Zacchaeus waved goodbye, he shouted, "And I don't mind being little – that was the way I got to meet you!"

*   *   *

Stimulus questions

1. Some people think that winning millions of pounds in the lottery will make them happy. Is this true? Why didn't Zacchaeus' money make him happy?
2. What shows that Zacchaeus was determined to meet Jesus?
3. What shows that he really meant to make a fresh start?
4. What do you think Zacchaeus asked Jesus that evening?

Thinking time

1. Think of what it must be like to have no friends at all. You may know someone who never seems to have friends to play with. What could you do to show that you are willing to be a friend?
2. Think of a time when you needed to make a fresh start. How did you feel?

Prayer

"Lord, when we see someone looking unhappy because they have no friends, show us what we can do to help them. When things have gone wrong give us courage to make a fresh start. Amen."

PETER'S FRESH START

Life can seem very difficult when you are eleven, and nearly twelve. That's just how Peter Robinson was feeling as he made his way home from school after football practice. The trouble was his parents! They were very good and he knew they really loved him as much as they did his two younger sisters, Sarah and Jemma. But they just didn't seem to understand what it was like to be nearly twelve. These days he never seemed to do anything that satisfied them. Half the time they criticised him for behaving like a child and reminded him that it was about time he grew up. Then when he wanted to do something that was really grown-up, like when he asked if he could have the latest mobile phone, they reminded him that he was only a child and that money didn't grow on trees. It wasn't as if he didn't help at home. He was quite sure that, because he was a boy and the eldest, he got all the nasty jobs to do. Sarah hardly seemed to do anything, and of course Jemma, being only six, couldn't do much anyway.

He arrived home to find his father in a bad mood. He wasn't often grumpy, but obviously something had happened to upset him. He was holding a letter that he had just opened.

"Come and have a look at this, Kate," he grumbled to his wife. "It's a rip-off!"

"Whatever is it that's making you so cross, Steve?" she asked.

"Only the bill from the plumber for fixing the shower," he replied.

"Well, Steve, you can't expect people to work for nothing – and you did keep saying you hadn't time to do it yourself!" she said, remembering how often he had promised to fix it himself.

"He's trying to charge £85.40 plus VAT – it only took him less than an hour. Do you know he's charged for every little thing – washers, screws, brackets, solder – you'd think he was rebuilding the house."

Peter went up to his room, leaving his father to rant and rave about the plumber's bill. But that gave Peter an idea. One of the problems of being nearly twelve was that he never had enough money for the things he just had to have. He remembered what his Mum had said: "You can't expect people to work for nothing!" If the plumber sent a bill to his father for the work he had done, why couldn't Peter send his parents a bill for the work he did? He set to work and thought of all the things he had done in the past week. He tore out a sheet of paper from a school exercise book and made out his bill:

BILL to Mr and Mrs Robinson for work done this week.

Babysitting for Jemma	£3.50
Tidying bedroom each day	£7.00
Washing up twice	£2.00
Clearing out garden shed	£4.00
Cleaning bike	£1.50
Helping Sarah with school project	£2.50
TOTAL	£20.50

He carefully folded the bill and put it in an envelope and left it on the mat by the front door. He felt very pleased with himself. He felt even more pleased with himself the next morning at breakfast when he found an envelope on his plate. As he opened it, out fell two £10 notes and 50p in coins. "Thanks, Mum and Dad," he said eagerly. They just stared at him blankly. He dashed upstairs to put his money away when he noticed another envelope that had been pushed under his bedroom door. He eagerly opened this one, but his face fell when he read it. It said:

BILL to Peter Robinson for work done this week.

Preparing seven breakfasts	£7.00
Preparing packed lunches	£5.00
Washing football kit	£3.50
Transport to school	£10.00
Car journey to swimming baths	£2.50
Repairing bike, new tyres and brakes	£12.75
Deposit for school camp	£25.00
TOTAL	£65.75

Peter gulped. "Wow! How am I going to be able to pay all that?" All the items were correct. He added it up again and it still came to £65.75. He never realised just how much his parents did for him and what it cost. He took it for granted that they did it because he was their son and loved him. Then he thought about his bill to his parents. He felt ashamed to think what he had done. He realised that he in turn should do things to help because they were his parents and had cared for him for nearly twelve years. So he wrote another note: "Dear Mum and Dad, I'm sorry I can't pay your bill all at once, but here is £20.50. Will this do? Can we talk about it all – I think I've been very silly. Love, Peter." He left the note with his parents' bill and the money on the dining-room table.

He wasn't looking forward to breakfast the next morning. Sarah and Jemma were tucking into their Weetabix, but Peter just sat quietly. His parents didn't say anything either. Then his father read Peter's note, and with the tiniest smile to Peter's Mum, he tore up his bill to Peter.

"I reckon £20.50 will do, Peter," he said. "Perhaps you're right about having a talk about things. Time we all made a fresh start."

Stimulus questions

1. Do you agree with Peter that parents sometimes expect you to be grown up and then remind you that you are still a child? Why is this? Can you give examples?
2. Had Peter got a point in making out a bill to his parents? What would be on your bill to your parents? What would be on their bill to you?
3. What do you think Peter and his parents talked about when they decided to make a fresh start?

Thinking time

1. Think of the things that you do at home to help your family. Then think of the things that they do for you. Which is the longer list?
2. Are there other things about which you would like to make a fresh start? Who can you trust to talk to about them?

Prayer

"Lord, forgive us when we get things wrong and do silly things. Give us courage to own up to them and to talk about them with someone we can trust. Help us to know how to make a fresh start when things go wrong. Amen."

PETER DENIES JESUS
LUKE 22:54-62

Telling the Truth
It takes great courage to tell the truth when you are afraid.

"And I promised faithfully that I would never leave him, even if all the others did. I even said that I was ready to go to prison with him or even to die for him – and look what I've done! I swore that I'd never even heard of Jesus! How could I do that? He did warn me that before the cock crowed I would deny him three times. What did he mean? And now they've taken him away and are going to crucify him! After all he has done for me."

Peter was in tears as he thought about the events of the last few days. Let's listen while he tells his story.

"Jesus had chosen me to be one of his disciples, along with my brother Andrew. We were fishermen and Jesus said he would show us how to catch people for God's kingdom. At first we didn't understand what he meant. We had been with him for about three years and seen some astonishing things – blind men getting their sight, lepers being made clean and the lame being able to walk again. I had even been present when he brought back to life a little girl of twelve. We slowly began to understand what he meant about catching people for God's kingdom.

"We eventually made our way to Jerusalem for our great religious festival of Passover, and it was there that things started to go wrong. The religious leaders were jealous that Jesus was so popular and they made a plan to get rid of him. At the beginning of the festival, Jesus had a special supper with us all, at which he said that he would be arrested and put to death. He then said a very strange thing – that he would rise again. It was then that I made my rash promise that I would never leave him and was even ready to die with him. But I always was one for opening my mouth without really thinking things through first.

"After that supper, we went to the Garden of Gethsemane, a quiet, peaceful place just outside the city walls. It was there that soldiers and Jewish leaders came and arrested him. I tried to defend him by striking the servant of the high priest with a sword. Fortunately, my aim was not too good – I cut off his right ear – otherwise I would have been guilty of murder.

"When they had arrested Jesus they took him off to the high priest's house. The other disciples fled for their lives, but I remembered my promise never to leave him, so I followed at a safe distance to see what would happen. The soldiers had made a fire in the courtyard and I sat down with them to warm myself, trying not to be noticed. I wondered what was going to happen to Jesus. Believe me, I was scared. 'Any minute now one of the soldiers is going to recognise me,' I thought to myself. But it was a servant girl, sitting with us by the fire, who said, 'This man was with him!' and they all turned to look at me. I was so scared I just shouted out, 'Woman, I don't know him.' A bit later someone else said, 'You are one of them.' 'Man, I'm not!' I snapped. About an hour later another of them saw my face in the firelight and said, 'This man was with Jesus for sure – you can tell he comes from up north in Galilee by the way he talks.' I have never been more terrified in all my life. 'I don't know what you're talking about,' I screamed in panic.

"It was just then that the cock crowed – and I understood what Jesus had said earlier. At the same time Jesus turned and looked straight at me. That was the worst moment of all – it was just as if a knife had pierced my heart. I had let him down at the very moment that he needed me. I was all talk and no action. After all he had done for me, I just hadn't the bottle to stay faithful to him. I couldn't bear it any longer. I got up and fled with tears streaming down my face. I wept and wept. Me, big strong Peter, the one Jesus had called The Rock. I had just melted like snow in front of a young servant girl. Well, that's me finished. I have had my chance and blown it. Whatever am I going to do now? I shall live the rest of my life with this terrible betrayal on my mind." Peter burst into tears again.

This wasn't quite the end of this sad story. Jesus was crucified and three days later he rose to life again, as he had said. Shortly afterwards, Jesus appeared to the disciples as they were fishing. Peter was with them, still feeling very sorry about what he had done. Jesus walked over to where Peter was standing all alone.

"Peter, do you love me?" asked Jesus.

"You know that I do, Lord," he replied, with a lump rising in his throat.

"Peter, do you really love me?" Jesus asked him again.

"Yes, Lord, I really do," pleaded Peter.

"Peter, do you really, really, love me?" Jesus asked him for the third time.

Peter could hardly contain himself. "Yes, Lord, you know that I do really love you!"

Jesus smiled at Peter and said to him, "Well then, Peter, I've still got a job for you to do. Go on catching people for the kingdom and making them strong in their faith."

Peter could hardly believe his ears. Jesus had forgiven him and given him another chance. Peter became one of the leaders of the Christian church. He had learned such a lot that would help other people to be followers of Jesus. He grew to have courage to tell the truth, even when he was scared and in great danger.

* * *

Stimulus questions

1. Why did Peter find it so hard to keep his promise never to leave Jesus? What had he done to try to help Jesus?
2. What do you imagine Jesus was thinking when he looked at Peter after he had said he didn't know him? Why did Peter find it hard to tell the truth?
3. How can you tell that Peter was really sorry for what he had done?
4. Why do you think Jesus asked Peter, "Do you love me?" three times?

Thinking time

1. Think of a time when you lied about something because you were scared. How did you feel? What were you able to do to put things right? How did you feel then?

Prayer

"Lord, help us to think carefully before we make promises, and then give us the courage and strength to keep our word. When we fail to tell the truth, give us more courage to admit it and ask for forgiveness. Amen."

PETER'S BIG TEST

THEME: **Telling the Truth**
It takes great courage to tell the truth and do what is right.

Peter Robinson had just left school for home when he remembered he had left his PE kit in the classroom. His mother had told him to bring it home for washing. As he turned to go into his classroom he noticed that the only person there was a boy called Kenny, who had only recently joined the school. Kenny was standing by the teacher's desk, holding a digital camera. When he saw Peter, Kenny looked startled and moved away, quickly stuffing the camera into his pocket.

"I didn't know you had a digital camera, Kenny," said Peter. "When did you get that?"

"Well, I have now," Kenny grunted, "and what's it to do with you, anyway?"

"Nothing, really," said Peter. "I've just come back for my PE kit."

"If you know what's good for you, you've seen nothing. Get it?" snapped Kenny.

Peter was about to get his PE kit and leave when he noticed Mrs Carter, the deputy head teacher, passing the door.

"Come on, you two, hurry up. Haven't you got homes to go to?" she said.

The following morning, when they were in the middle of maths, Mr Wright, Peter's class teacher, came over to Kenny and said in a grave voice, "Mr Wheeler, the head teacher, wants to see you at once." This was no great surprise; Kenny was always having to see the head teacher about something. He returned after about fifteen minutes and gave Peter a menacing look as he went back to his desk. "Now Mr Wheeler wants to see you, Peter," Mr Wright said, equally gravely. Peter was quite puzzled about this. He had no idea what it was about. He knocked on Mr Wheeler's door and went in when he heard the cheery "Come in!"

"Oh, it's you, Peter," Mr Wheeler said. "Come and sit down. I've something very serious to ask you. First thing this morning, Mr Wright reported to me that his digital camera was missing from his desk. Mrs Carter tells me that she saw you and Kenny alone in the classroom after school yesterday. What have you got to say?"

Peter swallowed hard. He felt himself turning red and beads of sweat already started to form on his brow. He felt sick inside and his heart started to beat faster. He was terrified. He knew that Kenny had threatened him if he said anything, but he knew deep down what he should do.

"I...I...I just went back to the classroom to get my PE kit," Peter spluttered.

"And was anyone else in the classroom?" probed Mr Wheeler.

"No! I just got my kit and went," replied Peter, choking on each word as he said it.

"Well, that's not what Kenny has just told me," Mr Wheeler said firmly. "He said that *he* had come back for *his* PE kit and saw you standing by Mr Wright's desk. This is a very serious matter, Peter. It's not like you to be involved in trouble. I should report this to the police at once, but Mr Wright has asked me to do nothing until tomorrow, to give you both time to think and then tell the truth. I'll give you both until tomorrow morning to tell me the truth."

Peter went home that afternoon feeling dreadful. He had lied to the head teacher, when he knew he should tell the truth; but he was scared stiff what Kenny would do if he did tell the truth. If he told the truth Mr Wheeler would know he had lied. How could he face his parents then? When he got home, his mother could tell at once that something was wrong, but he wouldn't say anything. His parents knew for sure that it was something serious when he didn't eat any tea, but sulkily went up to his room. That night he just couldn't get to sleep for thinking about what he was going to do. What would happen if he said nothing and Mr Wheeler informed the police? What would Kenny do to him if he did say something? He tossed and turned and felt quite ill. When his parents went to bed they heard him groaning and saying in his sleep, "What will he do to me if I tell?" They knew it was serious. His mother brought up a drink and his father gently roused him, though he wasn't really asleep.

"Come on, Peter," said his Dad quietly, "it can't be as bad as all that. What's the matter?"

"Have this drink while you tell us what's troubling you so much," added his mother.

Peter burst into tears and sobbed uncontrollably. He told them the whole story from the very beginning. When he calmed down a little his father said, "I'm going to ask you to do something that will take great courage, Peter, but I think you know it is the right thing to do. Don't be afraid, your Mum and I will be with you."

So next morning the three of them went to see Mr Wheeler at school. "I think Peter has something he would like to tell you, Mr Wheeler," said Peter's father. Very slowly and nervously Peter began to tell the true story. He had almost got to the end when Mr Wheeler's phone rang.

"Sorry, to interrupt you, Mr Wheeler," said the school secretary, "but I've got Kenny's mother on the phone saying he came home yesterday with a digital camera and won't tell her where he got it. She wants to know if you know anything about it."

"Thank you, Miss Bedford," replied Mr Wheeler. "Tell her I'll ring her back in five minutes."

After that the whole business was quickly sorted out. The camera was returned to Mr Wright, and Kenny was put on report for a week and had to spend every lunchtime clearing litter from the field. He was warned that if he did something like that again he would be suspended. Peter waited to see what his punishment would be for lying about the incident.

"I really think you have had your punishment already, Peter," said Mr Wheeler. "Remember, if you do something wrong and tell the truth, the punishment you get will be far less than if you try to lie about it. But I think you know that now. Let's hope that Kenny learns that lesson too."

Peter went away feeling very relieved. He had learned an important lesson, but it had taken a lot of courage to do the right thing. He had no further trouble from Kenny, who was learning his lesson the hard way.

* * *

Stimulus questions

1. Peter didn't want to lie, but he was scared of Kenny. Is there anything else he could have done? Have you ever been in a situation where you wanted to do one thing, but ended up doing something else?
2. Do you think Peter should have said something to Mrs Carter straight away?
3. What do you think of Peter's father's idea of Peter going with his Mum and Dad to see Mr Wheeler? Do you think that was the best idea? How do you think Peter felt about it?
4. What did Mr Wheeler mean when he said that Peter had had his punishment already? Should he have been given the same punishment as Kenny?

Thinking time

1. Think of a time when you have been too scared to tell the truth. How did you feel? How did things work out in the end? Did you have someone you could trust to talk to about it?

Prayer

"Lord, when we are too scared to tell the truth, give us courage to overcome our fear. Give us strength to talk about it to someone we can really trust. Amen."

THE ROAD TO EMMAUS
LUKE 24:13-35

THEME: **Sadness**

We often need courage to deal with sad things that happen.

"I just don't know what to make of it all," said a bewildered Cleopas to his wife, Judith. "I've never heard such fantastic things in all my life!"

"I know, dear, it does sound very odd," agreed Judith, "but Joanna and Mary and the others wouldn't just make it all up. They definitely got up very early and took spices and perfumes to the rock tomb where Jesus had been put after he had been crucified. They were very upset, as we all were, but they wanted to clean his body and make everything tidy after the terrible things that had happened to him."

"That's all well and good, but to come back with stories about finding the heavy stone rolled away from the mouth of the tomb and Jesus' body missing – well, it's crazy. It would take more than ten strong men to shift that stone," said Cleopas scornfully. "And besides that, they went on about seeing two men in gleaming white clothes, who told them that Jesus had risen – whatever that might mean."

"Well, you must admit that Jesus did say that he would rise again after he had been put to death," argued Judith. "I just can't think that they were making it all up."

"Yes, I do remember him saying something like that, but we were all so anxious and confused, it didn't seem to make any sense," said Cleopas, "and it still doesn't! Are you sure that they went to the right tomb?"

"Of course they did!" snapped Judith. "Didn't Peter go and

have a look for himself, just to check that they hadn't got things mixed up?"

"Sure he did," agreed Cleopas, "but he came back just as puzzled as the women. All he saw were the strips of cloth that Jesus had been wrapped in, but no sign of Jesus – or of men in gleaming clothes, for that matter. He had no idea what had happened."

So the two disciples of Jesus went on walking and talking about all that had happened that day. They had hurried to Jerusalem from their home in Emmaus, which was about seven miles away, as soon as they had heard that Jesus had been arrested. Now that Jesus had died, there seemed no point in staying any longer and were going home.

"It's a great pity that things had to end like this," sighed Cleopas. "We all thought that Jesus was going to do something great in Jerusalem, like setting up his own kingdom, but ever since Judas betrayed him to the authorities, everything went wrong."

"I know," agreed Judith, "but he did some wonderful things, like healing the sick and curing the blind and the lepers. I just can't think it will end like this."

They made their way wearily towards home, with their shoulders bowed in sadness and their heads looking down at the ground. They were not aware that someone was walking behind them, until he had caught them up and said, "What is it that you're talking about? You sound so sad."

"You must be the only person in Jerusalem who doesn't know what's been happening there these last few days," said Cleopas, glancing quickly at the stranger who had caught them up. He didn't realise that it was Jesus. In fact, Jesus was the very last person he expected to meet!

"What things do you mean?" asked the stranger.

"About Jesus of Nazareth," Cleopas explained. "He was a

great prophet and did marvellous things to help people. He had come to Jerusalem with his disciples and we thought he was going to set up his own kingdom and get rid of our Roman rulers, but he was betrayed by one of his own disciples and arrested. He ended up being crucified three days ago. What's made us more confused than ever is that some of our women friends went to his tomb early this morning and couldn't find his body. They came back with some crazy story about having seen angels who said that he was alive. Some of our friends also went to the tomb; it was just as the women had said, but they didn't see any sign of Jesus. We just don't know what to think."

"How silly you are," said the stranger, with a smile. "Don't you remember what all the prophets said – that God's Saviour would suffer and die, but that wouldn't be the end?" Then Jesus started to explain to them what the prophets had said in the Jewish writings about himself. Their hearts began to beat faster. Cleopas and Judith looked at each other, but didn't like to say anything. How did this stranger know all these things? They listened carefully to all he had to say. In no time at all they arrived back in Emmaus.

"Why don't you stay with us for a meal?" asked Judith. "It's getting late."

Jesus thanked them and they gathered round the kitchen table.

"Since you are our guest, will you say a prayer to thank God for our food?" asked Cleopas. Jesus took a loaf of bread, said a prayer of thanks, broke it and gave a piece to Judith and Cleopas. It was just as if a blindfold had been taken from their eyes!

"Jesus!" cried out Cleopas and Judith together, giving each other a hug. When they turned to look at Jesus again, he was gone.

"That explains the burning feeling we had on the way here – it was Jesus all the time. We just didn't look at him properly," Judith said.

"I knew it was Jesus as soon as he broke the bread," Cleopas said. "Don't you remember how he did it when he fed those 5,000 people?" Grabbing a few pieces of bread and cheese, Cleopas added, "Come on, we're going straight back to Jerusalem to tell the others." They ran almost all the seven miles and arrived quite out of breath. The disciples were thrilled to listen to their story.

"I know it's true," beamed Peter, "I've seen him as well. He is alive, just as he said."

They were so excited they spent all night exchanging stories about Jesus being alive.

* * *

Stimulus questions

1. What made the disciples so sad after the crucifixion of Jesus?
2. Have you ever been really upset about something that has happened?
3. Why do you think that Cleopas and Judith didn't recognise Jesus?
4. What do you think it was that made Cleopas and Judith realise it was Jesus?

Thinking time

1. Think of a time when you have been very upset by something that happened. How did you feel?
2. What things helped you to understand and accept it?
3. Think of a time when you were very excited about something. How did you feel?

Prayer

"Lord, when things happen to make us sad, give us courage and help us to understand. When good things happen, help us to share them with others. Amen."

WHERE IS GRANDMA ROBINSON NOW?

THEME: **Sadness**

Good things can come out of great sadness.

"Come and have a look at what we've found!" cried Jemma and her friends as they said "Hello!" to the visitor who had just come into their class.

Jemma Robinson was in the Year 2 class at King's Road Primary School and while they were quite used to having visitors, it was always nice to see someone else. They knew this visitor was a safe person to talk to because he was wearing a "visitor" badge. Their teacher, Miss Dexter, had explained that the visitor was an inspector, but the only inspector that Jemma knew about was the man who checked the tickets on the bus. Still, he seemed very nice, and at playtime he went with Jemma and her friends to the bottom of the school field.

"What is it that you want to show me?" said the inspector.

"It's a dead hedgehog!" replied Jemma, looking at him with wide eyes.

"He really is dead," said Amanda, poking the hedgehog gently with a stick.

"I wonder where he is now," said Jemma thoughtfully.

"He's there, of course, in the long grass," said Kate rather scornfully. "He isn't going to go very far now!"

"I don't mean that," said Jemma. "I know his body is there, but a hedgehog is more than just a ball of prickles."

"What do you mean by that?" asked the inspector.

"Well, we've seen this hedgehog lots of times and he's been such fun," Jemma explained. "We've seen him run across the field with his little feet going so fast, he pokes around in the leaves looking for worms with his snout and he loves to lap the milk we give him with his pink tongue. We've got to know him very well – he's really become our friend. He can't just have come to an end."

"Maybe he was ill. Now he's died he won't hurt any more," said Amanda. "Perhaps he's gone to the hedgehog heaven!"

"I'm not sure about that, but I think he will still live on in all the things you can remember about him," said the inspector with a wise nod of his head.

The bell rang for the end of playtime and they all hurried back to their class.

When Jemma got home she could hardly wait to tell her Mum and Dad the news.

"I've got some very sad news," she said in a very serious voice.

"Whatever is it, Jemma?" asked her mother.

"Our school hedgehog has died and we took the inspector to see it," she said.

Her elder sister Sarah looked sad, but Peter, who was nearly twelve, looked disappointed.

"A dead hedgehog! Is that all?" he said abruptly. "Is that so important?"

"Well, *I've* got some very sad news and it is important," said Mrs Robinson. "I think you had all better sit down while I explain. You know that Grandma Robinson has been very ill. Well, we have heard from Grandad that she had a fall and was rushed into hospital. Unfortunately, she died before they could help her."

The three children were silent and hung their heads. Peter tried hard to hold back a tear, but Sarah couldn't help crying. Little Jemma simply said, "Poor Grandad."

"Where is Grandma now?" said Sarah, wiping away a tear.

"She's still at the hospital," replied her mother.

"I don't mean that," went on Sarah. "Grandma can't just have ended."

"Oh, I see what you mean," said her mother with a comforting smile. "Well, you know that Grandma and Grandad are Christians, and so they are sure that Grandma is now in heaven, where there is no more pain and where she will be at peace."

"I believe that too, but she is *really* still alive," insisted Jemma.

"What do you mean by that?" asked Peter, looking rather puzzled.

"Well, it's just like the hedgehog," insisted Jemma. "The inspector said that the hedgehog will still live on in all the things we can remember about it. Grandma will still live on in all the good things we can remember about her."

"That's very sensible for a little girl who's only six," smiled her mother. "I'm glad you listened to what the inspector said. What good things can you remember about Grandma, I wonder?"

"I remember the time I was very silly and tried to run away from home," admitted Peter. "When I ran out of money and it rained, I went straight to Grandad's and Grandma's. They didn't get on at me, but listened to how I felt. Grandma really seemed to understand what it was like to be nearly twelve."

"I remember the time I had measles," said Sarah. "Grandma came over every day while you and Dad were at work. She read to me and played games. It was really quite good having measles. She was so kind."

"I remember the times she came with us to the caravan," said Jemma, not wanting to be left out. "When I wanted to paddle and build a sandcastle and you and Dad said you were too tired to help, Grandma always came with me. She said it reminded her of when she was little like me. I could never really think of Grandma being little like me. She always had lots of time to do things with me."

"So, Grandma will still live on in all the memories we have of her," said Dad.

"She will still live on in you," said Mum, "if you try to be as kind and understanding as she was." But this was a bit too hard for them to understand.

* * *

Stimulus questions

1. If you had been watching the dead hedgehog, what would you have said when Jemma said, "I wonder where he is now"?
2. What did the inspector mean when he said, "I think he will still live on in all the things you can remember about him." How could the hedgehog be dead and alive?
3. How did the children show that, in a way, their Grandma was still alive?
4. What did their Mum mean when she said, "She will still live on in you if you try to be as kind and understanding as she was"?

Thinking time

1. Have any of your grandparents, or someone else in your family died? How did you feel? Think of some good memories that you have about them.
2. Do they still live on in you, as you try to be like them?

Prayer

"Lord, help us to understand that it is quite normal to feel very sad when someone dies. Help them to stay alive in our hearts in the good memories we have about them. Help us to be like them in all the good things they said and did. Amen."